Let God Be GOD

A Study of the Attributes of God | Teacher Guide | Revised Edition

Mark Eckel

Purposeful Design Publications is the publishing division of the Association of Christian Schools International (ACSI) and is committed to the ministry of Christian school education, to enable Christian educators and schools worldwide to effectively prepare students for life. As the publisher of textbooks, trade books, and other educational resources within ACSI, Purposeful Design Publications strives to produce biblically sound materials that reflect Christian scholarship and stewardship and that address the identified needs of Christian schools around the world.

Printed in the United States of America

15 14 13 12 11   1 2 3 4 5 6 7

Eckel, Mark

    Let God be God: A study of the attributes of God

    Revised edition

    ISBN 978-1-58331-276-6   Teacher guide   Catalog #HBLGT

Designer: Mike Riester

Editor: John Conaway

Purposeful Design Publications

A Division of ACSI

PO Box 65130 • Colorado Springs, CO 80962-5130

Customer Service: 800/367-0798 • Website: www.acsi.org

Contents

Introduction to the Course

On January 7, 1855, Charles H. Spurgeon began his Sunday sermon with these words:

> It has been said by someone that "the proper study of mankind is man." I will not oppose the idea, but I believe it is equally true that … the proper study of a Christian is the Godhead. The highest science, the loftiest speculation, the mightiest philosophy, which can ever engage the attention of a child of God, is the name, the nature, the person, the work, the doings, and the existence of the great God whom he calls his Father. There is something exceedingly improving to the mind in a contemplation of the Divinity. It is a subject so vast, that all our thoughts are lost in its immensity; so deep, that our pride is drowned in its infinity…. No subject of contemplation will tend more to humble the mind, than thoughts of God….
>
> But while the subject humbles the mind it also expands it. He who often thinks of God, will have a larger mind than the man who simply plods around this narrow globe…. The most excellent study for expanding the soul, is the science of Christ, and him crucified, and the knowledge of the Godhead in the glorious Trinity. Nothing will so enlarge the intellect, nothing so magnify the whole soul of man, as a devout, earnest, continued investigation of the great subject of the Deity. And, whilst humbling and expanding, this subject is eminently consolatory…. I know nothing which can so comfort the soul; so calm the swelling billows of grief and sorrow; so speak peace to the winds of trial, as a devout musing upon the subject of the Godhead.

Spurgeon was not expressing a brand-new thought. He was repeating and reinforcing what Christians have enthusiastically recommended for almost 2,000 years. And no wonder! When we devote time and energy to know who God is, we are in agreement with the clear teaching of Scripture.

> This is what the Lord says:
> "Let not the wise man boast of his wisdom
>   or the strong man boast of his strength
>   or the rich man boast of his riches,
> but let him who boasts boast about this:
>   that he understands and knows me,
> that I am the Lord, who exercises kindness,
>   justice and righteousness on earth,
>   for in these I delight," declares the Lord.
>
> —Jeremiah 9:23–24

> Now this is eternal life: that they may know
> you, the only true God, and Jesus Christ,
> whom you have sent.
>
> —John 17:3

> I consider everything a loss compared to the
> surpassing greatness of knowing Christ Jesus
> my Lord.
>
> —Philippians 3:8

Let God Be GOD

Helping our students know God is the heart's desire of every Christian school educator. We encourage every teacher to emphasize—and demonstrate—the importance of a personal relationship with God. Christian teachers provide multiple opportunities and invitations for students to trust in Jesus Christ as their Savior and Lord. But we also know that the teacher can only do so much. We can provide inviting environments and be faithful witnesses, but we cannot orchestrate the faith decisions of our students. We can give guidance and direction to help students grow into faithful disciples of Jesus Christ, but we know that only as they yield to the work of the Holy Spirit will they "grow in the grace and knowledge of our Lord and Savior Jesus Christ" (2 Peter 3:18).

The goal of *Let God Be God* is to help eighth-grade students learn about God, whom we want them to know. J. I. Packer warns, "Disregard the study of God, and you sentence yourself to stumble and blunder through life blindfold … with no sense of direction and no understanding of what surrounds you. This way you can waste your life and lose your soul" (1973, 14–15).

There are many "gods" competing for the loyalty and devotion of our students; this course can help them differentiate the one true God from false gods. Your students will search the Scriptures to see what God has revealed about Himself. As Arthur W. Pink said, "An unknown God can neither be trusted, served, nor worshipped" (1975, 7).

As you teach this course, may God use you to lead many students to a deep personal knowledge of Him.

References

Packer, J. I. 1973. *Knowing God.* Downers Grove, IL: InterVarsity.

Pink, Arthur W. 1975. *The Attributes of God.* Grand Rapids, MI: Baker.

Spurgeon, Charles H. *Spurgeon's Sermons, Volume 1, 1855.* www.ccel.org/ccel/spurgeon/sermons01.txt

Course Outline

Following is an outline of this course:

Part I. The Knowledge of God Unit 1. Knowing God Unit 2. Describing God	In units 1 and 2, students address basic questions such as these: How can we know God? How can we describe God, or even talk about Him meaningfully?
Part II. The Trinity Unit 3. God Is One Unit 4. God Is Triune	In units 3 and 4, students wrestle with the doctrine of the Trinity—God is one and three. This core doctrine distinguishes the Christian faith from other belief systems; most "Christian" cults break from orthodox Christian teaching on this issue.
Part III. God's Unshared Attributes Unit 5. God Is Supreme and Self-Existent Unit 6. God Is Sovereign Unit 7. God Is Infinite Unit 8. God Is Immutable and Eternal Unit 9. God Is Incomprehensible and Ineffable Unit 10. God Is Omniscient and Omnipresent Unit 11. God Is Omnipotent	In units 5 through 11, students study attributes that speak to God's absolute uniqueness and supremacy. God is in a category by Himself; nothing and no one can be compared with Him (Isaiah 40:25).
Part IV. God's Shared Attributes Unit 12. God Is Good Unit 13. God Is Wise and Truthful Unit 14. God Is Holy and Righteous Unit 15. God Is Merciful and Just Unit 16. God Is Long-Suffering and Loving	Units 12 through 16 discuss God's communicable attributes—those characteristics (such as goodness, justice, and wisdom) that we can partially grasp by analogy with human experience—and that we are to reflect in our own lives.
Part V. Synthesis and Review Unit 17. God's Attributes: Complementary or Contradictory? Unit 18. Course Review, Final Exam, and Evaluation	Units 17 and 18 give students opportunities to digest, synthesize, and review what they have learned in the course. Unit 18 includes guidelines for developing a final exam.

Course Description

Let God Be God is a study of the nature and character of God. It is based on the premise that the more we know and understand God through a careful study of His Word, the greater will be our personal challenge to maintain a right relationship with Him. More than simply a body of information, the course translates knowledge into personal application as students discover how an attribute of God applies to daily life. Your students are faced with questions such as these: Why do we need to study the attributes of God? How do these facts about God affect me today? Why is this important to study? The answers your students uncover are what make this course unique. Day after day, they will integrate Scripture into their thinking as they face some tough questions about who God is and how He interacts with His creation.

This one-semester course is designed for eighth-grade students. Class members should each have a student activity book to complement their direct study of the Bible passages referenced. This teacher guide provides extensive suggestions for implementing the lessons day by day, including blackline masters and an evaluation system. The methodology involves students in the instructional process and extends to the application of biblical principles in their daily lives. A hands-on approach is used throughout.

How to Use This Guide

Instructional plan. This teacher guide provides a complete plan for your instructional program. It has been designed to facilitate your successful interaction with students as they study the attributes of God and apply what they learn to their lives.

Student materials. Each student should have the student activity book for this course and the version of the Bible adopted by your school. The student activity book provides "Interacts"— worksheets designed to assist students in their personal and group study of God's Word. To provide flexibility, the pages are punched for insertion into a 3-ring binder. They are also perforated for easy removal to give you the option of having students hand in some of them for grading. You have several options for using Interacts, including the following:

• assign a complete Interact to the entire class

• assign selected items to certain students

• assign selected items on specific days.

You will need to decide when it is appropriate to assign some or all Interact questions as homework, depending on the class time available and the pace of the course. Be sure to allow sufficient time in your schedule to respond to your students' work. The Interact questions serve as the basis for class discussion.

Days of instruction. Each unit is divided into five days. Typically, the first four days build on each other. The fifth day is provided for enrichment and review; the fifth day also includes a unit quiz. This plan allows you flexibility in designing your program. Some schools have chapel in lieu of Bible class one or two days a week. You may want to do a memory-work checkup one day. You may need to allow for field trips and other school events. The materials are flexible enough to fit into a variety of schedules.

The days of instruction are not linked to specific days of the week. You can decide to implement the lessons from Monday to Friday, or you may begin with day 1 on another day of the week. The materials were designed to assist you, not to impose a specific structure. Feel free to add to, delete, or modify any suggestions in order to make the program more appropriate for your particular classes from year to year.

Visual aids. The course includes a CD of blackline masters (BLMs) to aid you in your instructional program. These BLMs may be displayed or projected as visual aids or duplicated for distribution to students. Each BLM is clearly numbered for your reference. Answer keys to the BLMs and Interacts can be found at the end of this teacher guide.

Student evaluation. A unit quiz is provided for day 5 of every unit. You have the option of assigning individual Interacts as homework to be handed in. Each unit also contains a Scripture memory passage that can be used for assessment.

Lesson format. The lessons in this teacher guide follow a predictable pattern and contain common elements. This continuity is designed to help you quickly grasp the key concepts covered, the materials needed, the sequence of activities, and the instructional flow.

Content overview. The instructional units are grouped into five major divisions:
- Part I: The Knowledge of God (units 1–2)
- Part II: The Trinity (units 3–4)
- Part III: God's Unshared Attributes (units 5–11)
- Part IV: God's Shared Attributes (units 12–16)
- Part V: Synthesis and Review (units 17–18)

The first pages of each major division feature a detailed overview of the content to be covered in that part of the course. This content overview is designed to equip you to present and discuss the topics in those units. It will help you anticipate challenges, explain difficult concepts, and handle student questions and concerns. It will also provide suggestions for helping students internalize, appropriate, and apply the biblical teachings in those units.

Objectives. Clear objectives are provided for each lesson.

Lesson materials. This section alerts you to the materials you will use in the unit, including any blackline masters that need to be displayed or duplicated for distribution.

Memory passage. At the beginning of each unit, this teacher guide provides a suggested Bible memory passage. Since schools handle memory work in various ways, you may exercise any of several options including these: use the memory passage suggested, expand the memory selection to longer passages, have students memorize an entire Bible book during the semester, participate in a schoolwide Bible memory program, or coordinate with the memory program of your supporting church.

You are encouraged to incorporate the memory program into your instructional day and to make it as creative as possible. Read, discuss, and assign the verses on the first day of the unit. Use varied techniques to provide practice in the next three days. (For example, when calling the roll, have students respond with each successive word of the assigned passage.) Oral or written evaluation can occur on the fifth day. Students should be responsible for the accumulation of verses over time and should be ready to respond to questions related to the memory work as part of each evaluation point.

Teaching strategies. This section provides step-by-step procedures for each day's instruction. You have complete control over the flow of these procedures within the time allotted for your class. Do not hesitate to move an activity from one day to the next, reduce or expand an activity, or replace an activity entirely.

Summary. This is your Bible class. The course materials are meant to assist you. If they are to be effective, you need to plan carefully for each instructional unit. Several weeks before the semester begins, scan through the course materials to identify activities that may require special preparation or coordination with others. Begin planning for them now.

Whom God calls, He enables for the task. You have a special privilege in opening God's Word daily to your students. It is a challenge to maintain an enthusiasm and awe that will impact your students' attitude toward studying God's attributes. Of all the things we must do well in a Christian school, none compares with the Bible teacher's task. May God richly bless you as you present the wonderful words and works of God, which, as the Holy Spirit enables, bring life changes and eternal rewards.

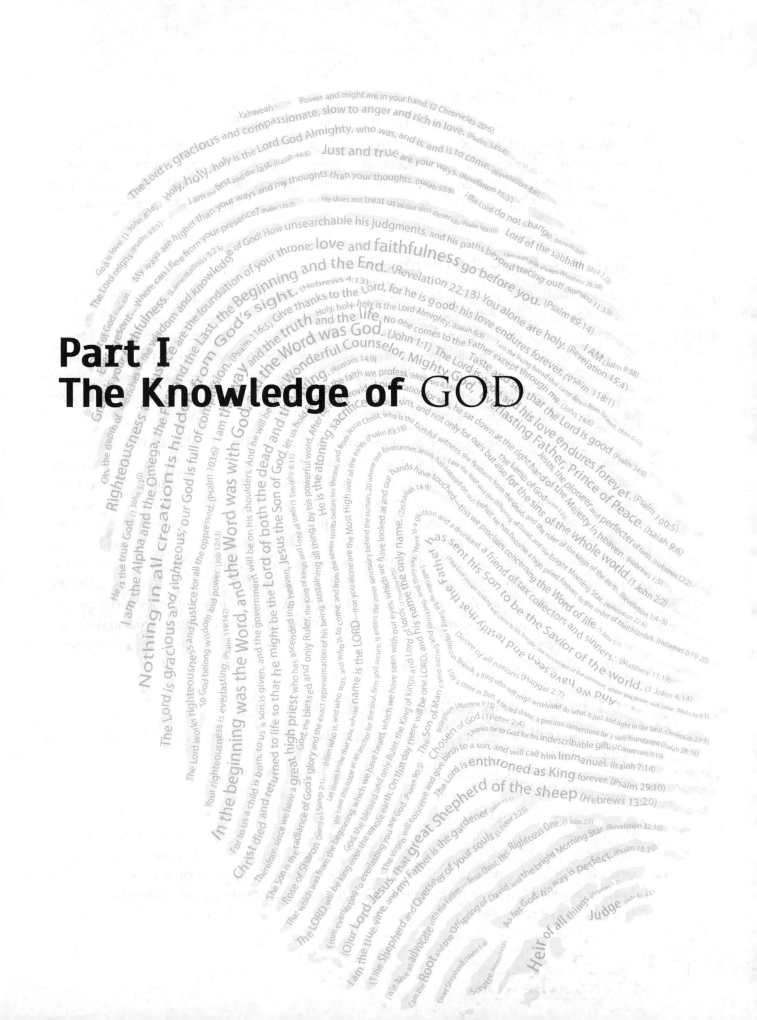

Part I
The Knowledge of GOD

Content Overview

The units in this section introduce students to two key facts about God: we can know God, and we can describe God. Though our knowledge of God and our ability to articulate that knowledge are extremely limited, they are adequate for us to know God the way He intended. "This is eternal life," said Jesus to His Father, "that they may know you, the only true God, and Jesus Christ, whom you have sent" (John 17:3). This content overview reviews some foundational truths regarding the important topic of the knowledge of God.

God Has Revealed Himself

God does not leave us to our speculations about who He is. Christian theologians distinguish between *general revelation* and *special revelation*. General revelation is available to every person everywhere through the normal human functions of observation and reason. The primary means of general revelation are nature (Romans 1:20) and conscience (Romans 2:14–15). However, just because God has revealed Himself in these ways does not mean that all people are aware of Him or that they are even searching for Him. General revelation is *available* to all, but people must be open to having God open their eyes to what He has revealed.

Special revelation includes every form of revelation other than general revelation. Though some attributes of God can be inferred from observing nature and thinking about what we observe, nature can't tell us that God is a Trinity, that God the Son became a man, that Jesus died to redeem us from our sins, and scores of other facts about God. Though human beings have a God-given awareness of right and wrong, the human conscience can't tell us the exact requirements of God's law, what sin is, what the consequences of sin are, the fact that our actions are subject to God's eternal judgment, or how to escape God's judgment. Most of the information we have about who God is, who we are, and how we can relate to God comes through special revelation. *The Bible is the primary source for special revelation.* Within the Bible, we read that God has revealed Himself in many specific ways— including audible speech, visions and dreams, and historical events (such as the Flood, the parting of the Red Sea, the Resurrection, and the life and teachings of Jesus). *The Bible gives us information about God that we can't acquire any other way.*

God Is Beyond Human Understanding

We can never fully understand God. He is incomprehensible. Paul presents this truth dramatically in Romans 11:33:

Oh, the depth of the riches of the wisdom and knowledge of God!

How unsearchable his judgments,

and his paths beyond tracing out!

However, we can know some things about Him, and we can know Him personally. Note the paradox in Ephesians 3:19. This verse is part of a prayer by the apostle Paul. He has already talked about God's love; in this verse he prays that the Ephesians will "know this love that surpasses knowledge"! Yet Paul is aware that whatever knowledge God gives us, at this point we only "know in part" (1 Corinthians 13:9).

Let God Be GOD

God Is Beyond Human Description

We cannot describe God in a way that exhausts all He is and all He does. However, we can describe certain characteristics of God. We cannot adequately describe God's character. Yet we can be accurate enough in our descriptions that, taken together, all these descriptions can give us an accurate concept of God. These descriptions of God's characteristics are called His *attributes*. The purpose of this course is to introduce your students to some of those attributes.

1 Knowing GOD

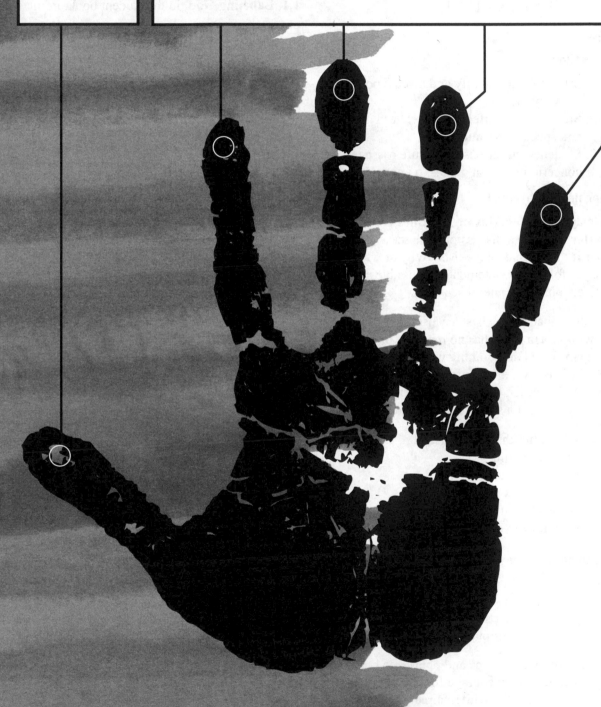

Unit 1 Knowing God

Memory Passage: Hebrews 11:6

Lesson Materials:
  Blackline Masters 1.1–1.3
  Interacts 1.1–1.4

Day 1

Objectives

1. Students will identify and discuss popular views of God.
2. Students will differentiate between general and special revelation.
3. Students will discuss Scripture passages concerning what it means to know God.

Teaching Strategy 1

Display **Blackline Master 1.1, Does God Matter?** Initiate a discussion with these questions: Does it matter that God exists? Why or why not? Use the following statements as possible answers or to encourage further discussion.

It matters that God exists because ...
  • without Him, life has no meaning or purpose.
  • apart from Him, nothing would exist.
  • otherwise, we are controlled by chance.
  • stability, order, purpose, and design are impossible without a self-existent, eternal Creator.

It doesn't matter that God exists if ...
  • I don't need Him.
  • I am my own god.
  • He is a figment of imagination.
  • He is dead, or ineffective in human lives.
  • God is in everyone and everything.

Teaching Strategy 2

Initiate a discussion with the following incomplete sentences. Use **Blackline Master 1.2, Who Is God?**
  • According to our society today, God is ...
  • According to Scripture, God is ...

Use the following words and phrases to complete the sentences and encourage further discussion:
  • a force, myself, a white-haired grandfather type in a rocker, the forces of nature, dead, a level of consciousness, a spiritual guide.

  • all-powerful, eternal, Creator, righteous, all-knowing, love, spirit.

Teaching Strategy 3

Have your students turn to the chart in **Interact 1.1, Labeling God**, in the student book. Point out that the names on the chart suggest views of God that some people hold today. Then lead your students in discussing each one. During the discussion, the students can start to fill in the chart, completing it later on their own.

Teaching Strategy 4

Discuss some of these questions to summarize the lesson:
  • What are some consequences of viewing God in a false way?
  • Do people really believe in a God who fits the descriptions in this activity?
  • Can you give any personal examples to illustrate one or more of these beliefs?
  • Can you think of any TV shows, magazine articles, poems, stories, novels, or songs that portray a God who is like any of these?
  • Do you think Scripture agrees with any of these images?

Day 2

Objectives

1. The students will evaluate biblically some popular views of God.
2. The students will discuss the possibility of defining God.
3. The students will consider the problems that arise when the creature tries to explain the Creator.

Teaching Strategy

Direct students to **Interact 1.2, Can We Define God?** in their student book. Allow about half the class time for them to complete this assignment on their own. Then discuss their answers. Student responses will reveal a lot about where students are on their spiritual journey.

Day 3

Objectives

1. The students will consider the question, How do we know anything?
2. The students will locate and record Scripture passages that will help answer the question, How can we know God?

Teaching Strategy 1

Begin with the question in the first objective: How do we know anything? Most answers will center around two ways: direct contact (personal experience, interaction, doing, using our five senses) and communication (listening to what others say, seeing films, reading books).

Ask your students to answer the question, How do people know about God? On the board, list the following three ways we can know about God, and discuss each one. Have your students explain and illustrate each way in which God shares knowledge about Himself:

- Natural revelation: the creation (Romans 1:19–20)
- Supernatural revelation: Jesus, the living Word (John 14:8–9)
- Scripture: the written Word (2 Peter 1:19)

Teaching Strategy 2

Have your students form small groups to look up the verses listed in **Interact 1.3, God Makes Himself Known**. Have them make notes as they consider each question. Afterward, use the prompts and suggestions in the answer key in this teacher guide as you discuss your students' observations. During the discussion, students may add to their notes.

Day 4

Objectives

1. The students will explore who God is and what He does as revealed in Genesis 1–3.

2. The students will learn to apply the O-I-C-A method of Bible study.

Teaching Strategy 1

Have your students label one sheet of paper *Who God Is* and another *What God Does*. Students may work individually or in small groups. They are to list things under each category, using only Genesis 1–3. For each characteristic or accomplishment listed, have them restate the verse in their own words with the citation immediately following. You may want to put the examples below on the board.

Who Is God? (Characteristics)

1. God exists.
   a. Genesis 1:1 begins with an assumption—God is.
   b. God is not made or created; humans are. (1:1, 26)
   c. God is separate from His creation. (1:1, 26–27)

2. God is eternal.
   a. Before the world was, God was. (1:1)
   b. Time began at creation. (1:1 "In the beginning ...")
   c. God can give eternal life. (3:22)

3. God is one, yet more than one.
   a. God. (1:1)
   b. "The Spirit of God." (1:2)
   c. "Let us make man in our image." (1:26–27)

4. God is perfect.
   a. Creation was God's idea, "good." (1:31)
   b. God established standards. (2:16–17)

5. God is powerful.
   a. God can do anything according to His character. (1:1)
   b. God created the world by Himself out of nothing. (1:1)
   c. God's power is supernatural and extraterrestrial. (1:1–2)

What Does God Do? (Accomplishments)

1. God creates.
   a. Creation is initiated by God. (1:l)
   b. All things are brought into being by God. (1:1)

2. God designs.
   a. God designs His plan for creation. (1:1)
   b. God's plan is orderly. (1:1–31)

3. God communicates.
   a. God speaks in order to create. (1:3, 1:6)
   b. God speaks with people. (2:16)
   c. God speaks with Himself. (1:26)
   d. God speaks with the serpent. (3:14)

4. God judges.
   a. God sets ethical standards. (2:16–17)
   b. God upholds ethical standards. (3:16–17)

5. God provides.
   a. God provides food for people. (1:29)
   b. God provides companionship. (2:18)

Teaching Strategy 2

Help your students complete **Interact 1.4, The O-I-C-A Method**. This Interact presents a common Bible study method that is sure to benefit your students. The process has four steps: observation, interpretation, correlation, and application (O-I-C-A). You might want to review the everyday meanings of these four words:
   1. observation: looking closely at what the text says
   2. interpretation: giving the meaning of the text
   3. correlation: showing how this text relates to other Scriptures
   4. application: putting the meaning into practice

Day 5

Enrichment Activities

1. Have students put together a mock TV drama or news report that illustrates how God works in the lives of people and in situations.

2. Have students keep a TV, radio, newspaper, or magazine log to record the times God is mentioned. Have them report how others describe who God is and what He does.

3. Have students conduct interviews with various members of the school staff. Have them ask questions like these:

   • What is the main cause of unbelief in God?
   • What satisfies people's spiritual hunger?
   • How do people become more mature spiritually?

Students can share their interview responses with the class.

4. Distribute **Blackline Master 1.3, Unit 1 Quiz**.

Let God Be GOD

2 Describing GOD

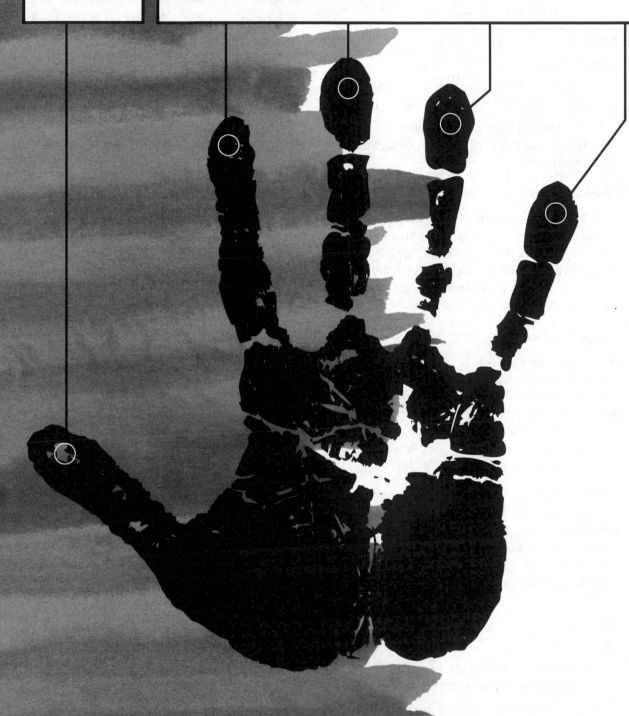

Unit 2 Describing God

Memory Passage: Jeremiah 9:23–24

Lesson Materials:

Blackline Masters 2.1–2.2
Interacts 2.1–2.2

Day 1
Objectives

1. The students will discover the attributes of God as revealed in a single chapter, Isaiah 40.

2. The students will create symbols representing the attributes of God to use as mnemonic devices.

Teaching Strategy 1

Introduce today's activities by asking the students to open their Bibles to Isaiah 40, explaining that this is one of the most revealing chapters in Scripture about God's attributes. Read the whole chapter aloud. Afterward, ask students what attributes they noticed and list them on the board.

Teaching Strategy 2

Invite students to find **Interact 2.1, God's Attributes**, in their student book. It lists all the attributes they will study in this course. Have them work independently or with a partner to fill in the chart with any attributes they find in Isaiah 40. Then use the answer key in this teacher guide as you discuss the chart with the class.

Let students know that by the end of the course, they will have filled it in completely. Duplicate and distribute **Blackline Master 2.1, God's Attributes**, and keep a supply available for students to work with. Encourage students to use this BLM as an overflow sheet for Interact 2.1.

Day 2
Objectives

1. The students will read a passage from Acts 17 and consider what it tells about God.

2. The students will discuss how God is related to His creation, including human beings.

Teaching Strategy 1

Have students look again at the chart for Interact 2.1, which they worked on yesterday. Read Isaiah 55:8–9. Ask, Why do we go to the trouble of trying to describe God if His thoughts and ways are so far beyond our ability to grasp? As students suggest answers, write them on the board. Then call students' attention to this unit's memory passage. We can't know everything about God, but He has given us the ability to know something; and God wants us to know as much as we can about Him. He also wants us to go beyond knowing about Him to knowing Him directly. Studying the attributes of God can help us know Him better.

Teaching Strategy 2

Direct students to **Interact 2.2, God and People**. Help them answer the questions provided, referring to the answer key for prompts. As students encounter specific attributes of God in Paul's speech, have them add those attributes to the chart on Interact 2.1. Call special attention to the second question on Interact 2.2. After Paul told the Athenians about God, he called on them to repent. Knowledge of God is not just information to be collected: it places a responsibility on the one who acquires it.

Day 3
Objectives

1. The students will read Psalm 103 and update their attributes chart.

2. The students will discuss their response to God's attributes.

Teaching Strategy 1

Have students turn to Psalm 103. Working individually or in groups of two or three, students will read the psalm several times, looking for specific attributes of God identified on Interact 2.1. Have them add those attributes to the chart. Assign Psalm 145 as homework. Have students look for attributes in that psalm and add those attributes to Interact 2.1.

Teaching Strategy 2

Ask students whether they think they're becoming

more skilled at seeing attributes of God in Scripture. Remind them that one of the main reasons for reading and studying the Bible is that God reveals information in the Bible that He doesn't communicate in any other way. If we want to know God better, we need to pay attention to the things He says about Himself in His Word. Ask students to look over the attributes they have added so far to Interact 2.1. Ask, If this is what God is like, how should I respond to Him? Encourage them to think of actions, words, attitudes, moral values, and other personal responses. Knowing God should make a difference in our lives!

Day 4

Objectives

1. The students will report on yesterday's homework assignment.
2. The students will discuss why it is important to learn about God's attributes.

Teaching Strategy 1

Have students turn to Psalm 145, and ask a student to read the whole psalm aloud. Ask students to share any attributes of God they found in this psalm. Write their answers on the board, along with the verse numbers where those attributes were found.

Teaching Strategy 2

Wrap up this unit with a discussion of why it is important to learn how to describe God. Call attention to the attributes coming up in unit 9: God is incomprehensible and ineffable. We can't understand Him completely, and we can't describe Him adequately. Those limitations don't mean we shouldn't do our best to understand God and describe Him, but it does mean that we should have the humility to admit that our knowledge and our descriptions are inadequate. We are finite; He is infinite. He is God; we are not. Yet God invites us to know Him. And knowing Him will keep us busy our entire life—and throughout eternity!

Day 5
Enrichment Activities

1. Divide the class into small groups. Have students search hymnbooks for hymns that mention attributes of God.

2. Assign various narrative sections of the Bible to groups of students—for example, the lives of Noah, Abraham, Sarah, Joseph, Moses, Deborah, Ruth, David, Daniel, Esther, or another Old Testament personality—and list attributes of God they find in those accounts. This could be challenging because students will not just be looking for attributes mentioned in the text; most attributes will need to be inferred from God's interaction with the characters.

3. Encourage tech-savvy students to use a database program to list as many attributes of God as possible and document Scripture locations for each attribute.

4. Distribute **Blackline Master 2.2, Unit 2 Quiz**.

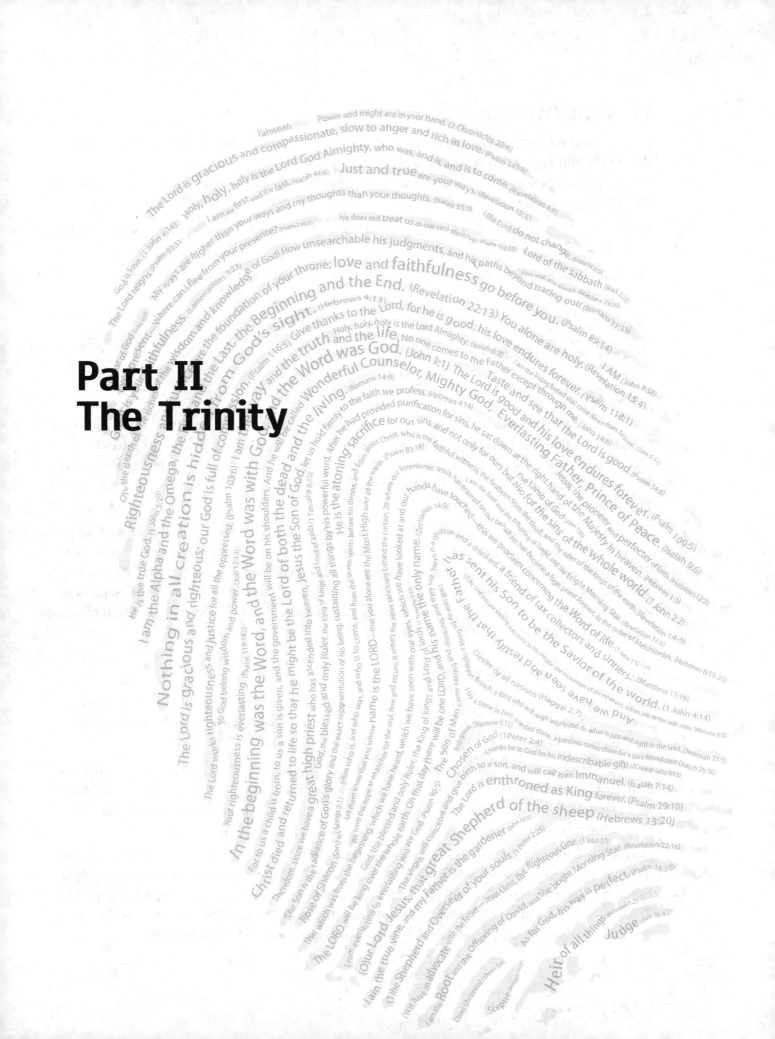

Part II
The Trinity

Content Overview

In unit 2 your students listed a number of attributes of God, and they will learn about many more in this course. But even if they listed hundreds of attributes, their knowledge of God would still be lacking. Attributes are characteristics that describe God, but they do not tell us that God—in His essence, in Himself—is one God in three persons.

In units 3 and 4, your students will not only learn that God is triune but will also begin to understand why this doctrine is central to the Christian faith.

The doctrine of the Trinity can be summarized in these three statements:

• God is one.

• God is three persons.

• Each of the persons is fully God.

God Is One

The *Shema*, found in Deuteronomy 6:4, is probably the best-known statement of God's oneness: "Hear, O Israel: The Lord our God, the Lord is one." Over the centuries, it became a creed for the Hebrew people. When a teacher of the law asked Jesus to identify the greatest commandment, Jesus prefaced His answer with the *Shema* (Mark 12:29). James links this doctrine with orthodox belief—a fact that even demons believe (James 2:19)!

The Bible affirms repeatedly that God is one. God is identified as the true God as opposed to false gods. He is one God, but there are many idols. People may trust in idols, but such false gods are powerless: "Turn to me and be saved, all you ends of the earth; for I am God, and there is no other" (Isaiah 45:22). This theme is continued in the New Testament. For example, when Paul spoke to the philosophers in Athens (Acts 17:22–31), he began by commenting on the many altars to many gods, and then proceeded to speak about the one true God.

God Is Three Persons

The first followers of Jesus were Jews, as were all the New Testament writers. (Luke was a converted Jew before he became a follower of Jesus.) It must have been a major shift for these early believers to see God as a Trinity!

In hindsight, we can see some indications in the Old Testament that within the one God there is some degree of plurality. But the only reason we have the concept that God is triune is because of a dramatic act of God. That act was the Incarnation. Jesus of Nazareth, a real human being, claimed to be God! How could this be?

During His life on earth, Jesus told His followers about His identity with the Father, His special mission on earth, His glorious existence before the Incarnation, and His future exaltation at the Father's right hand after His resurrection. Though the doctrine of the Trinity was not presented explicitly in the Old Testament, the God of the Old Testament is a Trinity. The writers of the New Testament books—especially the epistles—elaborated on Jesus' words and provided the first doctrinal writings we have on the subject of the Trinity. In the early centuries of the Christian church, as the doctrine came under fire from those who wanted to undermine it, the descriptions of the doctrine became more fully defined.

These two units won't answer all your students' questions about the Trinity. No matter how diligently they study—even after decades of thinking and reflection—there will still remain a great deal of mystery about the Trinity. Our finite minds can grasp this truth dimly at best (Isaiah 55:8–9), but God has revealed much of this truth to us. And what He has revealed is intended to strengthen us to do His will (Deuteronomy 29:29). The Trinity is essential to our understanding of who God is.

Help your students see units 3 and 4 as an introduction to who God really is in Himself. The doctrine of the Trinity pulls back the curtain and gives us a glimpse of God as He has existed for all eternity. The doctrine is a difficult academic problem, but we need to help students see it as much more than that. We want students to know God, not just know about Him. To know God is life eternal (John 17:3), and we will have all eternity to keep knowing Him better.

In several Bible passages, the three persons are mentioned together in a way that gives them equal status or suggests that the three names together represent God. Perhaps the most familiar example is part of what we know as the Great Commission: "Therefore go and make disciples of all nations, baptizing them in the name of the Father and of the Son and of the Holy Spirit" (Matthew 28:19). Notice that the word *name* is singular rather than plural. One name suggests one God; if Jesus had used the plural *names*, it would have suggested three gods.

Another example passage is 2 Corinthians 13:14: "May the grace of the Lord Jesus Christ, and the love of God, and the fellowship of the Holy Spirit be with you all." Paul is giving a blessing from the one true God, but he uses the names of three persons in the benediction. In Ephesians 2, Paul presents the good news that Jews and Gentiles have been made one through the death of Christ. Paul finishes this section with a summary statement that involves all three persons of the Trinity: "For through him [Christ] we both [Jews and Gentiles] have access to the Father by one Spirit" (2:18).

In these passages and others, the three persons are presented as distinct persons who have different functions and roles. (For example, see Matthew 3:16–17, 1 Corinthians 12:4–6, Ephesians 1:17, Ephesians 4:4–6, 1 Peter 1:2, and Jude 20–21.)

Each of the Persons Is Fully God

When theologians present the doctrine of the Trinity, their main approach is to point to the fact that Scripture describes each of the three persons—Father, Son, and Holy Spirit—in ways that are appropriate to God only. Following are just a few of the relevant passages.

The Father is God. The Father is presented in Scripture as the sovereign God, the creator of heaven and earth; "the Father" is a familiar name for God (Malachi 2:10). Jesus prayed to, and instructed His disciples to pray to, God the Father, who is Jesus' Father (Matthew 6:9, John 17:1). Paul also prayed to the Father (Ephesians 3:14).

The Son is God. John 1:1–3 says, "In the beginning was the Word, and the Word was with God, and the Word was God. He was with God in the beginning." In other words, the Word is both identical with God and distinct from God! This Word, "the One and Only," became flesh (1:14)—a clear reference to

Jesus—and this "One and Only" is God (1:18). In John 17:5, Jesus prayed, "Glorify me in your presence with the glory I had with you before the world began"—a glory that was not evident during Jesus' time on earth but which would be restored to Him after His resurrection and ascension (Hebrews 1:3). The Son and the Father are coeternal; therefore, they are both God. Other clear statements of the deity of Jesus can be found in Philippians 2:5–11, Colossians 1:15–20, and 1 John 5:20.

The Holy Spirit is God. The Holy Spirit is described in terms that can only apply to a person (1 Corinthians 2:10–12, John 16:13–14) who implements and applies the work of the Father and Son. In Acts 5:3–4, Peter declares that sinning against the Holy Spirit is sinning against God. The authors of Scripture were "carried along by the Holy Spirit." (2 Peter 1:21).

Why the Trinity Matters

When we speak of the Trinity, we're not just repeating an abstract truth that has been written into church creeds and confessions. We are dealing with the truth of who God really is in His person. The Trinity is not just a description of God; it is who He is. If He were not God in three persons, He would not be the God we love and worship.

The apostle John says that God is love (1 John 4:8). This phrase describes God's essential nature. God has been love from all eternity—long before He created the universe and the angels. He has never been lonely. He was under no compulsion to create, and He did not do so out of need (Acts 17:25). He has always been in relationship, even when there was nothing but God. The three persons of the Trinity—Father, Son, and Holy Spirit—relate to one another eternally in perfect love.

Another reason why the doctrine of the Trinity is essential is that without the Trinity, our atonement would be impossible. The book of Hebrews makes it clear that because Jesus is the holy, spotless, eternal Son of God, He alone is able to atone for our sins through His death. Jesus is the perfect high priest (Hebrews 4:14–16, 7:23–28), and His blood provides the only adequate sacrifice to atone for our sins (9:11–15, 10:11–14). A mere human being could not fulfill the roles of eternal high priest and sinless sacrifice; only God can be our Savior.

3

GOD **Is One**

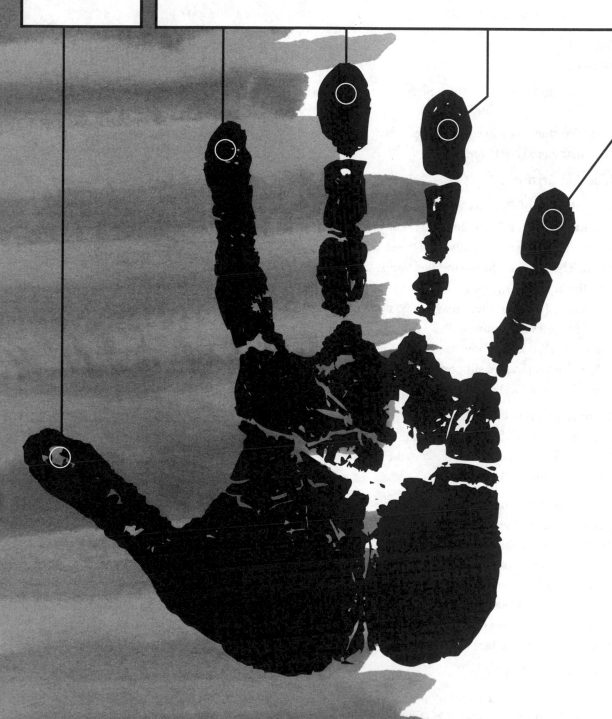

Unit 3 God Is One

Memory Passage: Deuteronomy 6:4–5

Lesson Materials:
  Blackline Masters 3.1–3.3
  Interacts 3.1–3.4

Day 1

Objectives

1. The students will analyze Scripture passages that affirm that God is one.

2. The students will explain why it is important that there is only one God.

Teaching Strategy 1

Write the text of Genesis 1:1 on the board, display **Blackline Master 3.1, Genesis 1:1**, or project the verse onto a screen. Ask students to read the verse aloud. Then ask the following questions. Don't rush the answers; give students time to meditate on the words so that their answers go below the familiar surface meanings.

• What can we learn about God from this verse?

• How does this verse support the fact that there is only one true God?

There is only one God. He created everything else that is not God. By implication, as the Creator, He is also sovereign over all of creation (Deuteronomy 10:14).

Remind students that at the time the book of Genesis was written, there were many religions that worshipped things in nature—animals, plants, sun, moon, stars, mountains, rivers, and so on. With that cultural context in mind, have students read the rest of Genesis 1. Ask them to explain how this account of creation reinforced to its original readers the fact that there is only one God.

Teaching Strategy 2

Write the text of Deuteronomy 6:4 on the board, display **Blackline Master 3.2, Deuteronomy 6:4**, or project the verse onto a screen. Ask students to read the verse aloud. Then ask the following

questions. Don't rush the answers; give students time to meditate on the words so that their answers go below the familiar surface meanings.

• What can we learn about God from this verse?

• How does this verse support the fact that there is only one true God?

• What does this verse say about how God relates to His people?

Depending on your time constraints, have students read the whole chapter, looking for verses and phrases supporting the fact that there is only one God. If your time is limited, call students' attention to verses 13–15. Ask students the following questions.

• Why do you think God made such a big deal of the fact that He is the only true God?

• How did God want that truth to affect the lives of His people?

Day 2

Objectives

1. The students will describe the differences between monotheism and polytheism.

2. The students will compile a collection of Scripture passages that talk about idols.

Teaching Strategy 1

Write the word *monotheism* on the left side of the board and *polytheism* on the right. (Use **Interact 3.1, Monotheism vs. Polytheism**, as your pattern.) Also add the center column of categories from that Interact. Use these categories as a lecture outline as you describe the differences between monotheism and polytheism. You may also decide to cover only a few of the categories in class and assign the others as homework.

Teaching Strategy 2

Have students turn to **Interact 3.2, God vs. "Gods" in Ancient Israel**. Remind them that the Israelites, after wandering in the desert for forty years, finally entered Canaan, where God commanded them to keep themselves separate from the people they found in the land. A look at the polytheistic Canaanite religions will help students understand why. As they work through Interact 3.2, they'll see parallels with today's culture in faith and life, in wrong ideas about God, and in sinful practices that result. Both ancient and modern cultures testify to the fact that the one true God is unlike any other "gods."

Assign the Scripture passages for individual students to find and read aloud at the appropriate time. Then lead the students in filling in their individual charts while you discuss what the Scripture tells us about God and the gods.

Day 3
Objectives

1. The students will explain why God condemns idolatry.
2. The students will contrast worship of God with worship of idols.
3. The students will identify some of the idols they encounter today.

Teaching Strategy 1

Divide the class into small groups. Ask students to turn to **Interact 3.3, Idols and Idol Makers**, and open their Bibles to Isaiah 44. Have each group read the Scripture passages and answer the questions. When most groups are finished, ask the groups to share their answers. Then discuss the findings as a class.

Teaching Strategy 2

Ask the students to turn to **Interact 3.4, The Dangers of Idolatry**. Have them look up the Scripture passages and fill in the worksheet. Students may work individually or in small groups.

Day 4
Objectives

1. The students will read and discuss passages in the New Testament that present the oneness of God.

2. The students will explain why it is significant that the New Testament writers believed that God is one.

Teaching Strategy 1

Assign Mark 12:28–34 to half the students and Acts 17:24–28 to the other half. Have them answer the following question about their assigned text: "What does this passage teach about who God is?"

As you discuss the passages with the students, emphasize the way each passage confirms the truth that God is one. If you have time, point students to 1 Corinthians 8:4, 1 Timothy 2:5, and James 2:19. Mention that 1 Timothy 2:5 is a good transition verse between this unit on the oneness of God and the next unit, which is about the Trinity.

Teaching Strategy 2

The followers of Jesus in the New Testament believed that God is one; however, it is in the New Testament that we find most of our information about the Trinity! Ask students to imagine what it might have been like for these people to begin changing the way they thought of God.

Day 5
Enrichment Activities

1. As in teaching strategy 1 of day 3, have students look up the verses on Interact 3.3, Idols and Idol Makers. However, instead of writing answers to the questions, have students summarize the teaching of Isaiah 44 in creative ways. For example, they may create a comic strip, draw a series of simple sketches, or perform short skits.

2. Someone has defined an idol as anything that we worship instead of God. Ask students to compile a list of things that people worship today. Lead a discussion about false gods in our society today.

3. Ask students to research some of the false gods that the Israelites encountered in

Canaan. Some examples are the Baals, the Ashtoreths, (Judges 10:6), Chemosh, and Molech (1 Kings 11:33). You may have students work in small groups and do research in reference books or online. What did people believe about these gods? How did they worship these gods? Why do you think God became so angry when His people worshipped these gods?

4. Distribute **Blackline Master 3.3, Unit 3 Quiz.**

4

GOD **Is Triune**

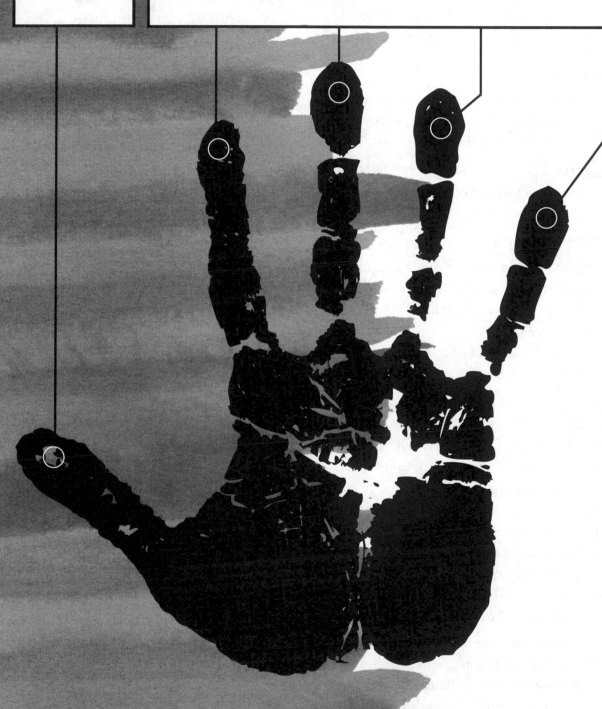

Unit 4 God Is Triune

Memory Passage: Ephesians 1:17

Lesson Materials:
Blackline Masters 4.1–4.2
Interacts 4.1–4.4

Day 1
Objectives

1. The students will identify passages of Scripture in which the three persons of the Trinity are mentioned together.

2. The students will establish that the New Testament writers taught that each member of the Trinity is God.

Teaching Strategy 1

Begin an introductory discussion by displaying **Blackline Master 4.1, The Trinity**, or by writing these statements on the board:

• There is one God.
• God is three persons: Father, Son, and Holy Spirit.
• Each of the persons is fully God.

Tell students that these three statements summarize the doctrine known as the Trinity. Also inform students that the word *trinity* is not found in the Bible. As students consider the three statements, prod their thinking with a few questions.

• How can all three of these statements be true?
• If the word *trinity* is not found in Scripture, why do Christians believe the doctrine?
• Do you believe in the Trinity? Why or why not?
• Is belief in the Trinity the same as belief in many gods (polytheism)?

Give the students time to think about their answers. Remember, this is introductory. Unanswered questions, different opinions, even discomfort about certain issues—these all help pave the way to future study of God's Word.

Teaching Strategy 2

Pose this so-what question: So what does the Trinity mean to us? Then ask: Why is it important that God is a Trinity? Isn't it enough that God is our Father? Following are some answers:

The Trinity is who God really is in His person. The Trinity is not just a description of God; it is who He is. He has existed from eternity as three persons; He did not start out one God and then become three persons.

The apostle John says that God is love (1 John 4:8). This phrase describes God's essential nature. God has been love from all eternity—long before He created the universe and the angels. He has never been lonely. He didn't create the universe because He needed someone to love, and the creation doesn't make God more complete or satisfy some need of His (Acts 17:25). He has always been in relationship, even when there was nothing but God. The three persons of the Trinity—Father, Son, and Holy Spirit—relate to one another in perfect, eternal love.

Without the Trinity, our atonement would be impossible. The book of Hebrews makes it clear that because Jesus is the holy, spotless, eternal Son of God, He alone is able to atone for our sins through His death. Jesus is the perfect high priest (Hebrews 4:14–16, 7:23–28), and His blood provides the only adequate sacrifice to atone for our sins (9:11–15, 10:11–14). A mere human being could not fulfill the roles of eternal high priest and sinless sacrifice; only one who is fully God can be our Savior.

Teaching Strategy 3

Direct students to **Interact 4.1, The Trinity**, in their student book. These verses will help the students understand basic biblical truths about the Trinity. To allow enough time for discussion, you might assign a limited number of verses to each student. Have students work independently, following the directions. Then discuss what the verses tell us about the Trinity. Refer to the answer key in this teacher guide for answers and ideas.

Day 2

Objective

The students will examine New Testament texts that present the Father as God.

Teaching Strategy 1

Have students turn to **Interact 4.2, God the Father**, in their student book. Divide the class into groups of two or three students. Give each group a Bible concordance or a Bible that contains a concordance. Have the students look up every New Testament mention of the Father or God. (In order to make the assignment more efficient and to avoid duplication of effort, you may wish to assign certain books to specific groups.) Have students write those references in the left-hand column. Then have them look up each verse and answer this question: How do these verses show that the Father is God?

Teaching Strategy 2

After students have completed the activity in teaching strategy 1, have them read through the verses again. This time, have them note beside each reference whether the Son (or Jesus or Christ) or the Holy Spirit (or the Spirit) is mentioned in that verse or in other verses nearby. At the end of the week, you and your students will compile these references into a chart documenting the New Testament references to the Trinity.

Day 3

Objective

The students will examine New Testament texts that present the Son as God.

Teaching Strategy 1

Have students turn to **Interact 4.3, God the Son**, in their student book. Divide the class into groups of two or three students. Give each group a Bible concordance or a Bible that contains a concordance. Have the students look up every New Testament mention of Son or Jesus or Christ.

(In order to make the assignment more efficient and to avoid duplication of effort, you may wish to assign certain books to specific groups.) Have students write those references in the left-hand column. Then have them look up each verse and answer this question: How do these verses show that the Son is God?

Teaching Strategy 2

After students have completed the activity in teaching strategy 1, have them read through the verses again. This time, have them note beside each reference whether the Father (or God) or the Holy Spirit (or the Spirit) is mentioned in that verse or in other verses nearby. At the end of the week, you and your students will compile these references into a chart documenting the New Testament references to the Trinity.

Day 4

Objective

The students will examine New Testament texts that present the Holy Spirit as God.

Teaching Strategy 1

Have students turn to **Interact 4.4, God the Holy Spirit**, in their student book. Divide the class into groups of two or three students. Give each group a Bible concordance or a Bible that contains a concordance. Have the students look up every New Testament mention of the Holy Spirit or the Spirit. (In order to make the assignment more efficient and to avoid duplication of effort, you may wish to assign certain books to specific groups.) Have students write those references in the left-hand column. Then have them look up each verse and answer this question: How do these verses show that the Holy Spirit is God?

Teaching Strategy 2

After students have completed the activity in teaching strategy 1, have them read through the verses again. This time, have them note beside each reference whether the Father (or God) or the Son (or Jesus or Christ) is mentioned in that verse or in other verses nearby. At the end of the week, you and your students will compile these references into a chart documenting the New Testament references to the Trinity.

Day 5
Enrichment Activities

1. Have students create a Trinity chart based on the New Testament. Using the data they collected during this week, students may display their findings on a large paper chart that will hang on a wall, or they may use a computer to create a table that can be projected.

2. Have students research the development of the doctrine of the Trinity in the early church, culminating in the Council of Nicaea and the Nicene and Athanasian Creeds.

3. Ask students to search for hymns and worship songs in which all three persons of the Trinity are mentioned. They can project the lyrics to several of these hymns and lead the other students in singing them.

4. Ask students to write their own Trinitarian lyrics to familiar tunes.

5. The Trinity is a paradox: one God, three persons, but not three Gods. Read aloud or display the following lines from the Athanasian Creed that relate to the Trinity, and discuss them with your students.

For there is one person of the Father, another of the Son, and another of the Holy Ghost. But the godhead of the Father, of the Son, and of the Holy Ghost is all one: the glory equal, the majesty coeternal. Such as the Father is, such is the Son, and such is the Holy Ghost. The Father uncreated, the Son uncreated, and the Holy Ghost uncreated. The Father unlimited, the Son unlimited, and the Holy Ghost unlimited. The Father eternal, the Son eternal, and the Holy Ghost eternal. And yet they are not three eternals, but one eternal. As also there are not three uncreated, nor three infinites, but one uncreated and one infinite. So likewise the Father is almighty, the Son almighty, and the Holy Ghost almighty. And yet they are not three almighties, but one almighty. So the Father is God, the Son is God, and the Holy Ghost is God. And yet they are not three Gods, but one God.

6. Distribute **Blackline Master 4.2, Unit 4 Quiz**.

Let God Be GOD

Part III
GOD's Unshared Attributes

Yahweah   Power and might are in your hand. (2 Chronicles 20:6)

The Lord is gracious and compassionate, slow to anger and rich in love. (Psalm 145:8)

Holy, holy, holy is the Lord God Almighty, who was, and is, and is to come. (Revelation 4:8)

Just and true are your ways. (Revelation 15:3)

I am the first and the last. (Isaiah 44:6)

God is love. (1 John 4:16)   My ways are higher than your ways and my thoughts than your thoughts. (Isaiah 55:9)   He does not treat us as our sins deserve. (Psalm 103:10)   the Lord do not change. (Malachi 3:6)

The Lord reigns. (Psalm 93:1)   Where can I flee from your presence? (Psalm 139:7)   How unsearchable his judgments, and his paths beyond tracing out! (Romans 11:33)   Lord of the Sabbath (Mark 2:28)

faithfulness. (Lamentations 3:23)   the wisdom and knowledge of God!   love and faithfulness go before you. (Psalm 89:14)   I am with you always. (Matthew 28:20)

On the depth of   the foundation of your throne;   the Beginning and the End. (Revelation 22:13) You alone are holy. (Revelation 15:4)   I AM (John 8:58)

Righteousness   God's sight, (Hebrews 4:13)   Give thanks to the Lord, for he is good; his love endures forever. (Psalm 118:1)

I am the Alpha and the Omega, the   (Psalm 116:5)   Holy, holy, holy is the Lord Almighty. (Isaiah 6:3)   I am the living bread that (John 6:51)

the way, and the truth and the life. No one comes to the Father except through   Taste and see   the Lord is good (Psalm 34:8)

Nothing in all creation is hidden from   and the Word was God. (John 1:1) The Lord is o   Wonderful Counselor, Mighty Go   sat down at the right hand of (Psalm 83:18)

He's the true God. (1 John 5:20)   (Romans 14:9)   the faith we profess, (Hebrews 4:1   the Lamb of God of the Majesty in heaven. (Hebrews 1:3)

I am the Alpha and the Omega, our God is full of co   He is the atoning sacrifice not only for ours but also for the sins of the whole world (1 John 2:2)

The Lord is gracious and righteous; our God is full of compassion. (Psalm 103:6)—I am the way   purifi   Jesus, the pioneer and perfecter of faith. (Hebrews 12:2)

Nothing in all creation   In the beginning was the Word, and the Word was with God   forerunner, Jesus, has entered on our behalf. He has become a high priest forever in the order of Melchizedek. (Hebrews 6:19-20)

The Lord works righteousness and justice for all the oppressed. (Psalm 103:6)   who has ascended into heaven, Jesus the Son of God, let us hold   I am the Root and the Offspring of David, and the bright Morning Star. (Revelation 22:16)

To God belong wisdom and power. (Job 12:13)   the Lord of both the dead and the   his powerful word. After   has sent his Son to be the Savior of the world. (1 John 4:14)

Your righteousness is everlasting. (Psalm 119:142)   a son is given, and the government will be on his shoulders. And he will be   and from Jesus Christ, who is the faithful witness, the firstborn from the dead, and the ruler of the kings of the earth. (Revelation 1:4-5)

For to us a child is born, to us a son is given   so that he might be the Lord   King of kings and Lord of lords (1 Timothy 6:15)   has a friend of tax collectors and sinners. (Matthew 11:19)

Christ died and returned to life so that he might be the Lord of both the dead and   And we have seen and testify that the Father   has a glutton and a drunkard, a friend of tax collectors and sinners. (Matthew 11:19)

Therefore, since we have a great high priest   God, the blessed and only Ruler, the King of kings and Lord of lords   Here I am   Desire of all nations (Haggai 2:7)

The Son is the radiance of God's glory and the exact representation of his being, sustaining all things by   (Him who is, and who was, and who is to come, and from the seven spirits before his throne, and   Here I am for David a righteous   I lay a stone in Zion, a tested stone, a precious cornerstone for a sure foundation (Isaiah 28:16)

Rose of Sharon (Song of Songs 2:1)   let them know that you, whose name is the LORD—that you alone are the Most High over all the earth. (Zechariah 14:9)   Thanks be to God for his indescribable gift! (2 Corinthians 9:15)

That which was from the beginning, which we have heard, which we have seen with our eyes, which we have looked at and our hands have touched—this we proclaim concerning the Word of life. (1 John 1:1)   and will call him Immanuel. (Isaiah 7:14)

The LORD will be king over the whole earth. On that day there will be one LORD, and his name the only name.   The Son of Man came eating and drinking   The Lord is enthroned as King forever. (Psalm 29:10)

From everlasting to everlasting you are God. (Psalm 90:2)   Chosen of God (1 Peter 2:4)   that great Shepherd of the sheep (Hebrews 13:20)

(O)ur Lord Jesus,   the virgin will conceive and give birth to a son   Bridegroom (Matthew 9:15)

God, the blessed and only Ruler, the whole earth.   I am the true vine, and my Father is the gardener. (John 15:1)

I am the Shepherd and Overseer of your souls (1 Peter 2:25)   Jesus Christ, the Righteous One. (1 John 2:1)   (Revelation 22:16)

(W)e have an advocate with the Father—Jesus Christ, the Righteous One. (1 John 2:1)   As for God, his way is perfect. (Psalm 18:30)

(T)he Shepherd and Overseer of your souls   I am the Root and the Offspring of David, and the bright Morning Star.   Judge (Acts 10:42)

Chief Shepherd (1 Peter 5:4)   Heir of all things (Hebrews 1:2)

Sceptre (Numbers 24:17)

Heir of all things

Content Overview

Theologians have traditionally divided the attributes of God into two broad categories: incommunicable and communicable attributes. (In this course we are using the terms *unshared* and *shared* attributes.)

The unshared attributes are those that are true of God alone. No human being is infinite or eternal, for example. There are other attributes that God shares with His creatures to some extent. For example, we are commanded to be wise, merciful, and just—in imitation of God. But these categories may not be as clear-cut as we might think. Though the word *wise* can be applied both to God and to us, the difference between the infinite perfection of God's wisdom and the finite imperfection of our wisdom can make us think the same word is used for two completely different things. Nevertheless, because God commands us to pattern our character after His by reflecting certain attributes, we can say that in some sense God shares those attributes with us.

In this course we will be examining the following unshared attributes of God: God is supreme, self-existent, sovereign, infinite, immutable, eternal, incomprehensible, ineffable, omniscient, omnipresent, and omnipotent.

Notice that some of these attributes use a negation to affirm a divine attribute. *Infinite* means "not finite"; *immutable* means "not changeable"; *incomprehensible* means "not understandable"; *ineffable* means "not describable." Our limited language simply doesn't have words that adequately convey these attributes; therefore, we use words that tell us what God is *not*. Other attributes use the prefix *omni-*, which means "all" or "universally": *omniscient* means "all-knowing"; *omnipresent* means "everywhere present"; *omnipotent* means "all-powerful." The other four attributes in our list—supreme, self-existent, sovereign, and eternal—suggest comparisons with created things.

The comparisons suggested by these words remind us of David's words in Psalm 145:3: "Great is the Lord and most worthy of praise; his greatness no one can fathom." But though we cannot fully comprehend God, we can still describe Him in meaningful ways. This course is intended to help your students do just that.

Following is a brief summary of the unshared attributes your students will be working with for the next seven units:

God Is Supreme and Self-Existent

To say that God is supreme is not just to say that He is greater and more powerful than false gods: He is the only God. No other being deserves to be called God. As the one who created and sustains all things, God has no equal. He shares His glory and majesty with no created thing.

God is uncreated; therefore, He is self-existent. He does not depend on any other thing for His existence; rather, all created things depend on Him.

God Is Sovereign

As the only God, the Creator who is supreme over all, God is absolute ruler, with absolute authority over all His creation. Nothing or no one can thwart His purposes.

God Is Infinite

God is without limit. Limitation comes with being created and defined. God the Creator defined every other thing simply by creating it. Not only is God without limit in His being, infinity also describes the perfection of every one of His attributes. He is infinite in love, wisdom, mercy, goodness, and so on.

God Is Immutable and Eternal

Change implies incompleteness or a lack. God has neither. His knowledge is infinite; therefore, he experiences no surprises or unexpected events. His plans are perfect from the time He conceives of them till they are completed. And His character does not change. No matter how many people rebel against Him or disobey Him, His love for them does not diminish or go away.

God is not subject to time constraints. He created a time-bound universe, and time itself. Every created thing has a beginning; the uncreated God has no beginning and no end.

God is Incomprehensible and Ineffable

Because God is infinite and we are finite, we can neither understand nor describe Him adequately. We know Him only to the extent that He has revealed Himself, and we must depend on His Word for guidance as to how to describe Him.

God Is Omniscient and Omnipresent

God possesses all knowledge. In essence, there are two types of beings: God and everything else. He has perfect knowledge of Himself, and He has perfect knowledge of everything else because He made everything else out of nothing.

God is everywhere fully present. God has no parts. When we say that God is with us, we don't mean that part of God is with us. God is infinite spirit. Other spirits (such as angels) can be present in only one place at a time because they are finite—limited. God has no such limitations.

God Is Omnipotent

God's almighty power is related to His supremacy and sovereignty. He has absolute authority, and He is able to exercise that authority. As the infinite God, He cannot be restrained by finite creatures.

Throughout the whole Bible, as people studied and meditated on these attributes of God, the normal responses were awe, worship, and obedience. We pray that your students will respond in these same ways.

5 | GOD Is Supreme and Self-Existent

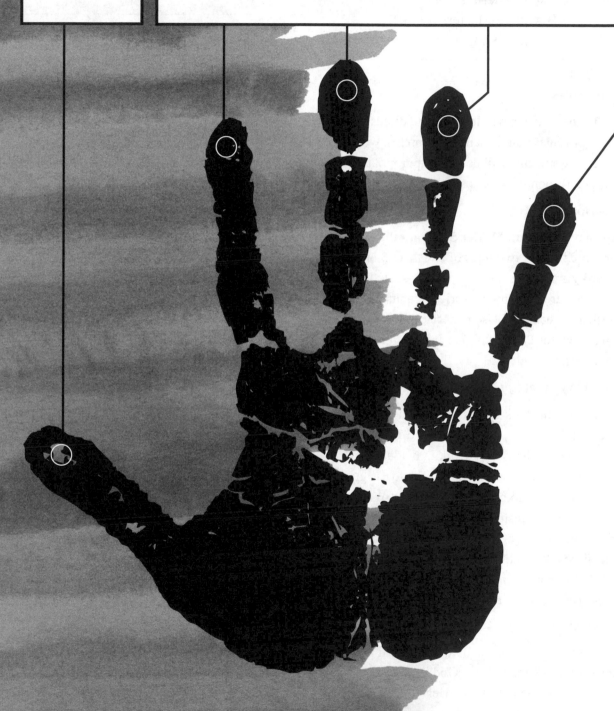

Let God Be GOD

Unit 5 God Is Supreme and Self-Existent

Memory Passage: Psalm 24:1–2

Lesson Materials:
Blackline Masters 5.1–5.2
Interacts 5.1–5.3

Day 1
Objectives

1. The students will look up and discuss Bible passages that declare the supremacy of God.
2. The students will describe appropriate ways to respond to God's supremacy.

Teaching Strategy 1

Display **Blackline Master 5.1, I am the Lord**, or write the first two lines of Isaiah 45:5 on the board. As students consider this verse, tell them that they are beginning a series of units on God's unshared attributes. Use material from the Content Overview for Part III to give a short introduction to units 5 through 11.

Teaching Strategy 2

Have students look up the verses and answer the first two questions in **Interact 5.1, God Is Supreme**. Students may work individually or in small groups. You may also wish to assign a portion of the Interact to each group. When students have finished the Interact, have them share their answers with the class. As you lead the discussion, call attention to the other divine attributes that are linked to God's supremacy in these passages (or in the context).

Teaching Strategy 3

Ask students to suggest answers to the third question in Interact 5.1: If God is supreme, how should we respond to Him? Help students see that the most common response in the Bible to God's supremacy is worship, and worship leads to obedience. The purpose of this exercise is to reinforce the truth that our goal in learning about God's attributes isn't merely knowledge for its own sake. We want students to know God, not just know about Him; and knowing God should cause profound personal change.

Day 2
Objectives

1. The students will list and discuss some personal implications of God's supremacy.
2. The students will describe why it is important for Christians to know that God is supreme.

Teaching Strategy 1

Have students turn to **Interact 5.2, God's Supremacy Matters**, and open their Bibles to Psalm 118. You may divide the class into groups of two or three to work on this Interact. Note that some of the questions on this Interact are very personal. You may want to give students the option of not answering some of the questions aloud if you think that may be an issue. You may also want to have students answer the first few questions in class and complete the others as homework. After the students have completed the in-class work, lead a discussion about why the Bible places such a strong emphasis on God's supremacy.

Teaching Strategy 2

Choose just a few passages from Interact 5.2 and lead the whole class in answering the questions. Discuss what this passage teaches about God's supremacy. Ask what other people think is most important—or supreme. You might phrase the question in terms of sources of information: What would TV advertisers say is supreme in life? What would political leaders say is supreme in this country or in the world?

Day 3
Objectives

1. The students will attempt to portray what existed before the creation of the world.

2. The students will explain why it is important that God is self-existent.

Teaching Strategy 1

Have students turn to **Interact 5.3, Before Genesis 1:1**. Ask students to respond to the first question. They may create a written description or a visual representation. When students have finished, ask them to read or display their creative work, one at a time. When all have had a chance to share their work, lead a discussion on God's self-existence. God depends on no one for His existence; He was under no requirement to create, and making the universe did not fulfill some lack in Him. He has no deficiencies, and never has had any.

Teaching Strategy 2

After the students have shared their responses to the first question on Interact 5.3, ask individual students to look up the verses in question 2. Ask students how these verses add depth to their response to question 1. Make notes on the board as students respond. Conclude the discussion by asking why it is important for God to be self-existent.

Day 4
Objectives

1. The students will correlate the attributes of supremacy and self-existence.
2. The students will collaborate on projects that communicate God's supremacy and self-existence.

Teaching Strategy 1

Divide the class into groups of three or four students. Have the students review their answers to Interacts 5.1, 5.2, and 5.3. As the students discuss these Interacts, one student in each group can summarize the main points on a separate sheet of paper. Give students a specific time limit for this activity. When the time is up, ask the recorders to share their summaries with the class.

Make notes on the board while the recorders are sharing. When all groups have responded, ask the class how the attributes of God's supremacy and self-existence are related.

Teaching Strategy 2

Divide the class into groups of four or five students. Have each group produce a communication vehicle—essay, story, picture, PowerPoint, skit, video, whatever—to explain God's supremacy, His self-existence, and how the two attributes are related. Students should begin by identifying the target audience (for example, young children, classmates, family members). Give students class time both today and tomorrow for working on the project. At the end of the day tomorrow, give students a chance to demonstrate their masterpieces.

Day 5
Enrichment Activities

1. Give students time to complete the communication projects they started yesterday (day 4, teaching strategy 2).

2. Bring in several systematic theology books. Distribute them to groups of students to leaf through. After they've reviewed the books for 20 or 30 minutes, ask for their impressions. Inform them that Christians have been creating such works for hundreds of years. They represent Christian attempts to understand what God has revealed about Himself.

3. Have students review what they've learned about God's supremacy and self-existence and add that information to Interact 2.1, God's Attributes.

4. Distribute **Blackline Master 5.2, Unit 5 Quiz**.

6

GOD **Is Sovereign**

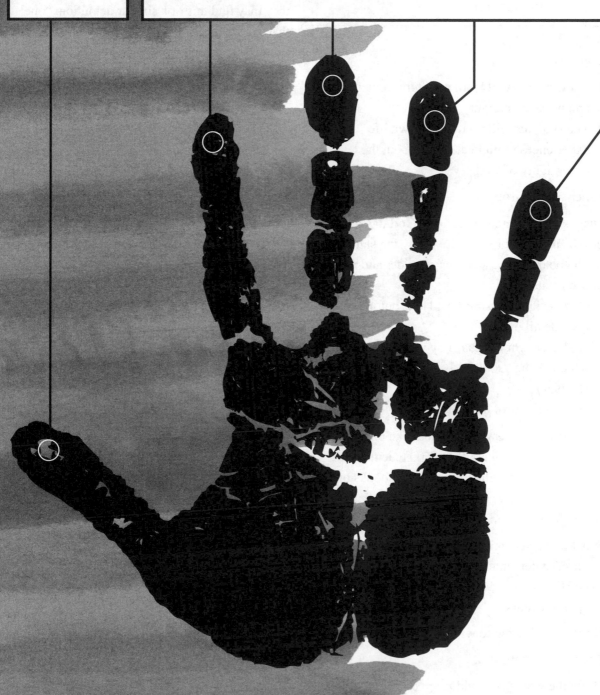

Let God Be GOD

Unit 6 God Is Sovereign

Memory Passage: Psalm 24:7–10

Lesson Materials:
Blackline Masters 6.1–6.5
Interact 6.1

Day 1

Objectives

1. The students will learn scriptural principles about the sovereignty of God.
2. The students will relate their own life experiences to biblical truths about the sovereignty of God.

Teaching Strategy 1

Display **Blackline Master 6.1, God designs possibilities ...**, or write the following statements on the board. Have students consider and respond to each statement:

1. God designs possibilities; He is not interested in each detail of life.
2. God is caught off guard by world situations, which change so quickly that He must change His plans.
3. Humans control their own destiny.

Ask, Have you heard comments like these? If so, where did you hear them? If students can't think of sources right away, suggest books or magazines, social media websites, popular song lyrics, or television programs.

What do these comments suggest? Bring out that all three statements suggest that God is detached from His creation and that He has no control over people or events.

Does the Bible agree with these comments?

Teaching Strategy 2

Write the words *rein* and *reign* on the board. Ask what each word means. Then ask whether the students see a similarity in the two meanings. Bring out that both words have to do with bringing someone (or something) under the rule or authority of another.

Add *sove-* in front of *reign*, forming the word *sovereign*, and ask students to define the new word. If necessary, have them check a dictionary, where they may find this or a similar definition: "one that exercises supreme authority within a limited sphere" (Merriam-Webster's Collegiate Dictionary, 11th Edition). The queen (or king) of England is a sovereign (or was until England's monarchs became "figurehead" rulers of a constitutional state, lacking real power to govern). Ask what we mean when we say that God is sovereign. God has absolute authority. Nothing happens that is outside His will and ability to control. Also, He is sovereign everywhere, for His "sphere," unlike that of any earthly sovereign, is unlimited.

Teaching Strategy 3

Direct students to **Interact 6.1, God Is Sovereign**, in their student book. Have them look up each passage and tell what it says about God's interaction with creation, people, and events. If you wish, divide the work, assigning selected Scriptures to individuals or groups, who will report to the whole class later so that all students can complete the Interact. Portions of this Interact may also be assigned as homework.

As students are completing their Scripture search, display **Blackline Master 6.2, If God is not sovereign ...**, or write the quotation on the board.* Ask students to comment on this quotation.

Teaching Strategy 4

Describe a time in your own life when you did not understand why something happened the way it did. Encourage a discussion among your students, asking them to tell about a similar event in their lives. Highlight the theme of Joseph's words: "You intended to harm me, but God intended it for good" (Genesis 50:20).

Day 2
Objectives

1. The students will define *sovereignty* and *providence*.
2. The students will apply biblical principles on sovereignty to their everyday lives.

Teaching Strategy 1

Display **Blackline Master 6.3, Sovereignty and Providence**, or write the words *sovereignty* and *providence* on the board.

Sovereignty: God has everything under control. (There are no emergencies in heaven.)

Providence: God cares for and personally oversees all events. (There is no accident or coincidence, no chance or luck, with God.)

Teaching Strategy 2

Display **Blackline Master 6.4, Personal Questions About God's Sovereignty**, and ask the following questions for discussion in large or small groups. Some students might prefer to make their personal application in writing—in a journal or another medium.

• Are there areas in my life in which I resist God's sovereign control? What are they?

• What would it be like if God were not involved in who I am? Would I prefer it that way?

• If God is in control of all things, why does He allow bad things to happen?

Day 3
Objectives

1. The students will examine problems that arise in Scripture about God's working in the world.
2. The students will begin to wrestle with the relationship between God's sovereignty and human freedom.

Teaching Strategy

Have students turn once more to Interact 6.1. Ask whether they discovered any problems or whether they discussed any difficult questions as they were completing the Interact. Here are two ancient questions related to this topic:

• How can both God and humans be responsible for an event?

• How can God be responsible for what seem to be negative events?

(You may want to comment that this teaching is not meant to frustrate students but rather to encourage them to think independently about what Scripture says.)

In response, display Blackline Master 6.2 and ask the following questions:

• Is anything not under the control of God? If you answer yes, what alternatives are possible?

Bring out the following:

Determinism/Fatalism. Things are predetermined by blind force.

Chance/Anarchy. There are no laws except those I create, or pretend are true. The result is chaos.

• What about human choice? What about human skill or effort? If humans do not have ultimate control, do we have any control over the outcome of an event—an athletic contest, for instance? Review Proverbs 19:21 and 21:30. Now read verses like 21:5, 15:22, and 20:18. Our planning and diligence are crucial to the outcome of anything. Ultimately, however, God's sovereignty reigns regarding His eternal purposes.

• If we cannot understand this, why should we study it?

We should appreciate the mystery and tension in Scripture. Finite beings are not able to define or comprehend the infinite. As we have seen, if we could understand God, He wouldn't be God (Job 42:1–6; Isaiah 46:9–11, 55:8–9; Romans 11:33–36). God's ways are, for us humans, "unsearchable" and "beyond tracing out."

• Since God is sovereign, must we conclude that humans are puppets, responsive only to the strings of the puppeteer—God?

Absolutely not. Choices were made by the first humans in Genesis 3, and these choices still plague their descendants today. The consequences of these actions are still being passed on from generation to generation (Genesis 5:1, 3; Psalms 51:5, 58:3; Romans 5:12). The same is true of our decisions. Ultimately, however, the work of God is beyond our comprehension (Romans 9:14–21).

Day 4
Objectives

1. The students will study the life of Job as an example of how to respond to God's sovereignty.
2. The students will apply Job's example to their own experiences.

Teaching Strategy 1

Have students read Job 1–2. During or after their reading, have them observe in their notes how Satan is controlled by God. Their answers should reflect the following:
• Satan had to come to God.
• Satan had to ask for God's permission.
• Satan's actions were limited by God.
• Although Satan is directly orchestrating the evil events, God is ultimately responsible for allowing them to happen.
• In all that happened, God had a higher purpose, a bigger plan that was unknown to Job and others. But Job knew that God's plan was good. In Job 23:10, he says, "But He knows the way that I take; when He has tested me, I shall come forth as gold."

Teaching Strategy 2

Have your students read Job 38–42. These are the chapters in which God responds to Job's question, "Why is this happening when I have done nothing wrong?" Ask the following questions:

• Did God answer Job's questions?

No, not directly.

• What did God say?

He asked questions He knew Job couldn't answer.

• Why did God respond to Job in this way?

God was showing Job that His plans were beyond Job's comprehension and that Job had no right to ask why—and probably wouldn't understand the reasons anyway!

• When Job had an opportunity to speak, what did he say?

Read Job 40:3–5 and 42:1–6. Job was reminded of his position before God. He was finite and God was infinite.

Teaching Strategy 3

Recount a personal experience or ask students to relate personal events that ask the question, "Why do these things happen?" Highlight the theme again. Then go back to Job 1–2, and ask the students to find Job's two responses. What can we learn from these?
• Job acknowledged that God owed him nothing and could not sin.
• Job said that we must accept both the good and the bad.

Conclude the class by reading the following verses:

"And we know that in all things God works for the good of those who love him, who have been called according to his purpose." (Romans 8:28)

"The Lord is righteous in all his ways and loving toward all he has made." (Psalm 145:17)

Day 5
Enrichment Activities

1. Have students read and comment on James 5:10–11, the only New Testament reference to Job. Give opportunity for students to talk about their own experiences with suffering and ask how these verses from James might help in those situations.

2. Ask students to respond to the fact of God's sovereignty. How does it make them feel? What questions or difficulties do they have with God's sovereignty? How could they explain God's sovereignty to someone else?

3. Have students review what they've learned about God's sovereignty and add that information to Interact 2.1, God's Attributes.

4. Distribute **Blackline Master 6.5, Unit 6 Quiz**.

*Sproul, R. C., *Now, That's a Good Question!*, Wheaton, IL: Tyndale (1996), 26.

7 GOD Is Infinite

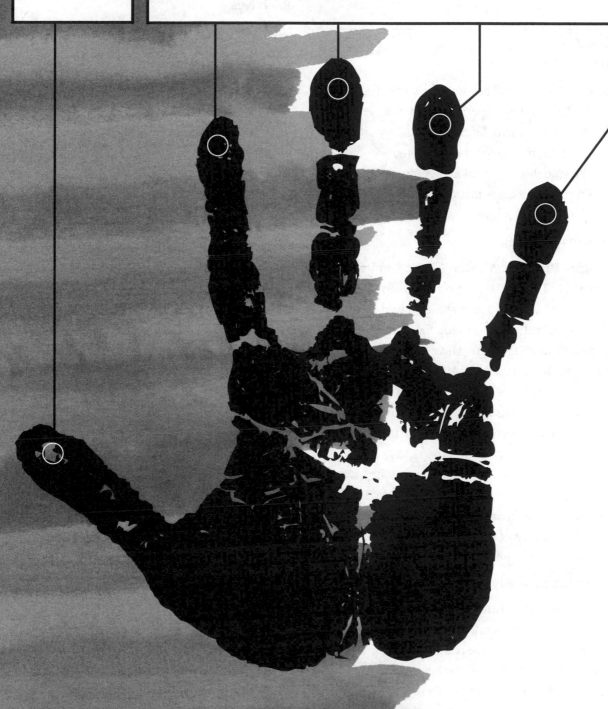

Let God Be GOD

Unit 7 God Is Infinite

Memory Passage: 2 Chronicles 2:5–6

Lesson Materials:
Blackline Masters 7.1–7.2
Interacts 7.1–7.3

Day 1
Objectives

1. The students will accumulate a list of limitations they experience and observe.
2. The students will describe imaginary situations in which they have no limitations.
3. The students will read and comment on Scripture passages that describe some ways in which God is infinite.

Teaching Strategy 1

Display **Blackline Master 7.1, No Limits**, or write "No Limits!" on the board. Keep it displayed during this activity. Have students turn to **Interact 7.1, My Limitations**. Divide the class into groups of two or three students. Have students answer the first question on the Interact by accumulating lists of things that place limits on them. Give students a time limit for this activity. When time is up, ask each group to share its answers. List the answers on the board. After all the groups have shared, ask several students to describe what they would like to do if they had no limitations. Note those answers on the board as well. Inform students that the purpose of this activity is to prepare their thinking for this unit's attribute of God: infinity.

Teaching Strategy 2

Refer students to **Interact 7.2, God Is Infinite**. The students may work individually or in groups to look up the Scripture passages and answer the questions. However, because of the nature of the material and because there are only a few references, you may wish to walk the whole class through the Interact together. As you discuss the Interact, help students work with the two main meanings of *infinite* as applied to God: "unlimited" and "perfect."

Day 2
Objectives

1. The students will link infinity to some of God's other attributes.
2. The students will begin a project related to God's infinity.

Teaching Strategy 1

Have students turn to the table of contents in the front of their student books. Point out that the attributes in units 7 through 11 are examples of the "unlimited" meaning of *infinite* (unlimited power, knowledge, duration, and so on); those in units 12 through 16 are examples of the "perfect" meaning (perfect in love, mercy, goodness, and so on).

Teaching Strategy 2

As students review the table of contents in their student books, ask them to choose one of the attributes from units 12 through 16. For the next two days they will research that attribute and relate it to infinity. Have students take notes on separate sheets of paper and record the results of their research on **Interact 7.3, God's Infinite Attributes**. If you have in-class Bible concordances, dictionaries, encyclopedias, or handbooks, make them available to the students. If you have Internet access, some students may wish to use Bible reference websites. You may wish to have students rotate from one resource to another to give other students access to limited resources and to give students experience with a variety of Bible study tools.

Day 3
Objective

The students will continue to work on their infinity projects.

Teaching Strategy

The students will continue to work on Interact 7.3. Establish rules for rotating from one study resource to another. Remind students that they'll learn more about God's shared attributes beginning in unit 12. The purpose of this project is to show the difference that infinity makes. Students should finish their projects by the end of the class so they can hand them in or present them tomorrow—whichever you decide.

Day 4
Objectives

1. The students will hand in or present their completed infinity projects..
2. The students will discuss some implications of the fact that God is infinite.

Teaching Strategy 1

Ask several students to present the results of their infinity projects to the class. If you have time for only a few presentations, make sure the projects cover different attributes. After the presentations are completed, have students hand in their completed projects.

Teaching Strategy 2

Ask the students how many infinitely large beings (or how many infinitely powerful beings) can exist at the same time. Ask students not to answer the question unless they can give a reason for their answer. Without comment, let several students answer the question and give their reasons. When a number of students have answered—or even if none have attempted to answer—mention the concept of limitation. If an infinite being is by definition unlimited, a second infinite being would limit that being, which means that the first being would not be infinite! What this means is that infinity not only affects the other attributes but also relates to who God is in Himself. Your students have already learned that there is only one God. God is supreme over all created things and does not depend on anything else for His existence. He is the sovereign Lord. If He were not infinite, those statements about God would not be true. He is the only infinite being.

Day 5
Enrichment Activities

1. How does the Trinity relate to infinity? If God is infinite, and He exists in three persons, does that mean that there are three infinites? Read aloud or display the following excerpt from the Athanasian Creed that relates to the Trinity, and discuss it with your students. The bottom line: there is one infinite God who exists in three persons—not three infinites, because that would mean that there are three gods!

   For there is one person of the Father, another of the Son, and another of the Holy Ghost. But the godhead of the Father, of the Son, and of the Holy Ghost is all one: the glory equal, the majesty coeternal. Such as the Father is, such is the Son, and such is the Holy Ghost. The Father uncreated, the Son uncreated, and the Holy Ghost uncreated. The Father unlimited, the Son unlimited, and the Holy Ghost unlimited. The Father eternal, the Son eternal, and the Holy Ghost eternal. And yet they are not three eternals, but one eternal. As also there are not three uncreated, nor three infinites, but one uncreated and one infinite. So likewise the Father is almighty, the Son almighty, and the Holy Ghost almighty. And yet they are not three almighties, but one almighty. So the Father is God, the Son is God, and the Holy Ghost is God. And yet they are not three Gods, but one God.

2. Have students review what they've learned about God's infinity and add that information to Interact 2.1, God's Attributes.

3. Distribute **Blackline Master 7.2, Unit 7 Quiz.**

8   GOD **Is Immutable and Eternal**

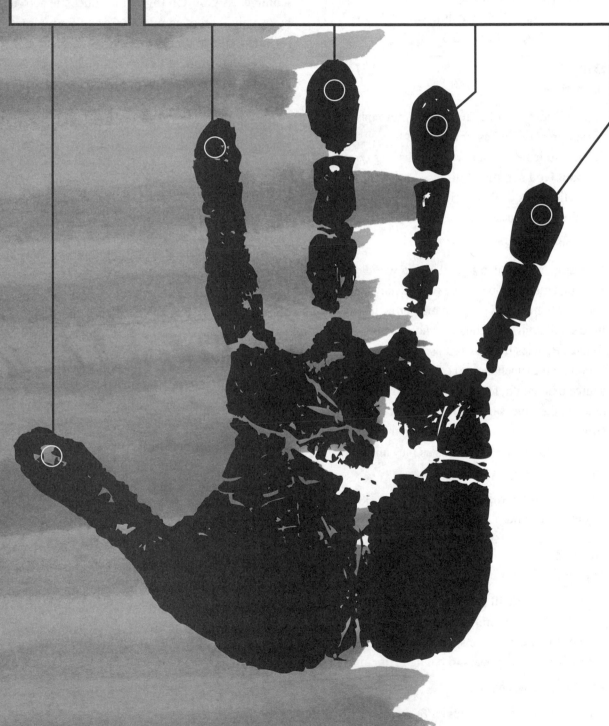

Unit 8 God Is Immutable and Eternal

Memory Passage: Isaiah 46:9–11

Lesson Materials:
Blackline Masters 8.1–8.2
Interacts 8.1–8.3

Day 1
Objectives

1. The students will examine Scripture passages that present God as immutable.
2. The students will answer and discuss questions about God's immutability, considering the implications of this attribute for society and for individual Christians.

Teaching Strategy

Your students live in a fast-changing world. For example, many people move often to new jobs and new homes, and children may grow up with little stability in their church, school, and circle of friends. Perhaps because of this, knowing that God is immutable (unchanging) can become a special source of strength, for He is indeed an anchor that holds in the storms of life. Have the students turn to **Interact 8.1, God Is Immutable**, in their student book and follow the directions as they answer questions relating to this attribute.

Discuss their answers, using the answer key on the CD for ideas and prompts.

Day 2
Objectives

1. The students will review and conclude their study of God's immutability.
2. The students will consider passages of Scripture in which God appears to change His mind.

Teaching Strategy 1

Have students review Interact 8.1, contrasting the changelessness of God with the changeableness of the human condition. Remind them that realizing God is immutable can help them know how to live their own lives.

Teaching Strategy 2

With the whole class, discuss **Interact 8.2, Can a Changeless God Change?** Introduce the activity by explaining that some passages of Scripture seem to indicate directly or indirectly that God "changed His mind." Invite volunteers to read aloud Genesis 6:6, Jonah 3:10, and Genesis 18:16–33 as examples. Then ask, In light of God's immutability, how should we understand these statements? (See also 1 Chronicles 21:1–15 and Jeremiah 26:3, 19.)

Explain that the Hebrew word used in these instances is *nahum* (na-cume). It means "a breath" or "a sigh," and thus shows an emotional concern expressed as compassion or grief. The NIV translates these passages properly. The KJV uses the word *repented*, seeming to say that God went back on His previous word. The Living Bible, a paraphrase, incorrectly states that "God changed His mind."

Explain that what may seem to us a divine adjustment or a deviation from the original plan is correctly interpreted as a divine action beyond our limited comprehension. (See Job 11:7–9, 42:1–6; Isaiah 40:13–14, 55:6–13; Romans 11:33–36; and Ephesians 1:9–11.) Often this is understood as anthropomorphism—a description in human terms of something that's not human (in this case, God). What these passages do is remind us that it is sometimes impossible to interpret in human terms the actions of an infinite God: " 'For my thoughts are not your thoughts, neither are your ways my ways,' declares the Lord. 'As the heavens are higher than the earth, so are my ways higher than your ways and my thoughts than your thoughts.' "

Day 3
Objectives

1. The students will examine Scriptures showing that God is eternal.

2. The students will answer questions and solve problems relating to this attribute.

Teaching Strategy 1

Direct students to **Interact 8.3, God Is Eternal**, in their student book. Have them follow the directions, working alone or in small groups. Afterward, use the answer key on the CD as you lead the class in discussing the answers.

Teaching Strategy 2

After discussing Interact 8.3, remind students that we live in a temporal world, and our time is limited. Ask them to think about these questions: Do I ever struggle with the use of my time? If so, how? Is it possible to bring this area of my life under submission to God? What active, personal, measurable tactics can I use to control my time?

Read Colossians 3:1–4 aloud. Suggest that students take time now to list their daily activities, asking this about each: How does this activity glorify God and help to prepare me for eternity? Should it take more (or less) of my time?

Day 4
Objectives

1. The students will synthesize in a mock newspaper their ideas about time-bound humans and our eternal God.
2. The students will compare and contrast God's eternal viewpoint and our limited human viewpoint regarding time.

Teaching Strategy 1

Display or duplicate **Blackline Master 8.1, Timeless**, a parody of a news magazine or newspaper. Point out that the page contains articles having to do with time and eternity, as well as special features, such as an obituary column and an advertisement. Explain that students will create their own class newspaper about time and eternity. They should complete their paper by the end of tomorrow's class.

Take a few minutes for students to brainstorm ideas for features not shown in the example, such as editorials, classified ads, sports news, financial news, technology, photos, comics, fashion, and food. Students may choose whatever kind of feature they'd like to do; they can work individually or with a partner. Each piece should reflect a scriptural principle or should be followed by relevant Bible verses in parentheses. Display the sample so that students can refer to it for ideas on content or layout.

Teaching Strategy 2

To help students get started on the newspaper project, encourage them to use a Bible concordance to find verses having to do with time and eternity. Encourage them to think about the implications of an eternal God and temporal humans. Provide quotation books or websites. Have students brainstorm familiar sayings and slogans ("Time flies when you're having fun," "Time is of the essence," "No time like the present") as well as titles (*The Time Machine*, *From Here to Eternity*) and phrases ("time warp," "time marches on," "on time"). Finally, help students develop a list of headlines to spark writing ideas. For example:

Minding Your Minutes

Turning Back the Clock

Time-Saving Devices

Perfect Timing

Twinkle Time

Your Time, His Hands

Right on Time

One a Day, Two a Day

Understanding the Times

These Are the Times That ...

Just a Minute

Don't Miss Your Appointment

Wait Your Turn

Day 5

Enrichment Activities

1. Take your students to a library or suggest websites to research topics that relate to eternal life and people's search for it. Themes might include reincarnation, cryogenics (the freezing of bodies to preserve them for a future time, when they will be brought back to life), or immortality. Discuss what was found and how it relates to the fact that God is eternal.

2. Continue work on the newspaper project from day 4. Consider printing and distributing this newspaper within the school and community. Be sure to save copies from year to year.

3. Have students review what they've learned about God's immutability and eternity and add that information to Interact 2.1, God's Attributes.

4. Distribute **Blackline Master 8.2, Unit 8 Quiz**.

Let God Be GOD

9 GOD **Is Incomprehensible and Ineffable**

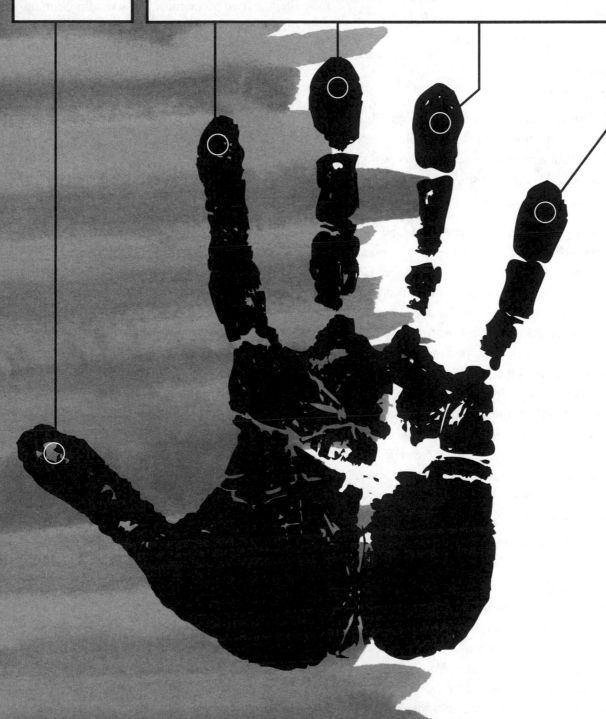

55

Let God Be GOD

Unit 9 God Is Incomprehensible and Ineffable

Memory Passage: Romans 11:33–36

Lesson Materials:

Blackline Masters 9.1–9.2
Interacts 9.1–9.4

Day 1

Objectives

1. The students will read and discuss Bible texts on the incomprehensibility of God.
2. The students will present various responses to God's incomprehensibility.

Teaching Strategy 1

Display **Blackline Master 9.1, If God Is Incomprehensible ...**, and lead a discussion of the statement. (Note: When we say that God is incomprehensible, we *don't* mean that we can know *nothing* about Him. We mean that we can't understand him *fully* or exhaustively or completely.) You may want to have students review some of the material in units 4 and 7 (on the Trinity and God's infinity) to reinforce the fact of God's incomprehensibility. Once that fact has been established, have students consider the second clause on the BLM. We can profit from a study of God because even though we can't completely comprehend Him, He has revealed a great deal about Himself.

Teaching Strategy 2

Have students turn to **Interact 9.1, Knowing the Unknowable**. Write the Scripture references from the Interact on the board or project them on a screen: Ephesians 1:17b–19, Jeremiah 9:23–24, John 17:3, and Philippians 3:8. Read and discuss each passage, one at a time. You may wish to divide the class into groups and have one group read and discuss each passage. Students may take notes on the Interact. All of these passages encourage us to know God better, even though He is ultimately incomprehensible! When all the passages have been discussed, ask the question, How should God's incomprehensibility affect the way we study the Bible? Encourage students to write some of the class responses on the Interact for future reference. Perhaps two of the most important implications of this attribute for Bible study are humility and dependence on God as we study.

Day 2

Objectives

1. The students will list facts they can know about God.
2. The students will begin to accumulate a list of names for God found in the Bible.

Teaching Strategy 1

Have students turn to **Interact 9.2, I Can Know God**. The book of Psalms is divided into five books: Book I, Psalms 1–41; Book II, Psalms 42–72; Book III, Psalms 73–89; Book IV, Psalms 90–106; and Book V, Psalms 107–150. Divide the class into five groups, and assign one of the books to each group. Have students read through their assigned psalms, looking for facts that fit in the columns on the Interact. A group may divide up its assigned psalms among its members, or the whole group may work through the psalms together. Students will continue to work on this Interact tomorrow.

Teaching Strategy 2

Have students research some of the names for God found in the Bible. They may use Bible reference works (Bible handbooks, dictionaries, encyclopedias, etc.) or do Internet searches. They can list their findings on Interact 9.2 or on other paper. They can complete the project in class or finish it at home. As students share their findings, create a list on the board or on a flipchart. The objective is not to come up with an exhaustive list; however, when students see how many items are on the list, they should be encouraged to know that even though they can't know everything about God, He has revealed a great deal about Himself.

Day 3
Objectives

1. The students will link the concepts *incomprehensible* and *ineffable*.
2. The students will compare some of the ways God is described in the Bible.

Teaching Strategy 1

Lead the class through a descriptive exercise. Tell them that you want to describe a human being. (Don't base this exercise on a real person!) Have students turn to **Interact 9.3, Picture a Person**. Go down the list of characteristics, one item at a time, and ask students to suggest an answer for each one. Randomly choose one of the suggested answers, and write that characteristic on the board. Students may fill in the figure on their Interact or simply use the Interact for notes. After you have led the class through the exercise, give students a few minutes to study the characteristics on the board. Then ask several questions to pull together the activity:

• Do you think you'd recognize this person on the street?
• Do you think you'd like to know this person?
• Would this person be a good friend?
• What are some things you still don't know about this person?

Allow several answers to each question. Then ask, If we still don't know everything about a human being after getting this much information, how much do you think we can know about God? Tell students that getting to know God is a never-ending project. Also, it can be difficult to find words to describe even what we do know about God.

Teaching Strategy 2

Divide the class into groups of two or three, or have students do this exercise individually. Have students turn to **Interact 9.4, Describing God's**

Love. On this Interact, Scripture passages are organized in categories representing different types of writing (literary genres). Assign the categories and passages to different students or groups. Ask them to read the passages several times; then they are to write what their assigned passages say about God's love. After the students have finished writing, ask them to share their answers. Call students' attention to the different ways the Bible talks about God's love, depending on the type of writing being used. But even with such a wide variety of writing types, the authors of the Bible still haven't said all there is to say about God's love! After all, even though the Bible is divinely inspired, it was written for finite human beings, who aren't able to understand God completely.

Day 4
Objectives

1. The students will summarize what they've learned about God so far in this course.
2. The students will establish personal attitudes for the remainder of this course in light of the fact that God is incomprehensible and ineffable.

Teaching Strategy 1

Have students leaf through the Interacts they have completed so far in this course. Ask students to mention any new facts they have learned about God in this course or any facts that they've understood in a new way. Make note of these on the board for the benefit of others in the class. Inform students that what they're experiencing is normal. Every time we study the Bible we are opening ourselves up to learning more about God, and this knowledge can lead us to know Him more personally. You might share an example from your own life that illustrates how your increased awareness of God's attributes has deepened your relationship with God.

Let God Be GOD

Teaching Strategy 2

Remind students of what they've learned in the last few days. Have them review Interacts 9.1–9.4 to refresh their memories. They have now completed about half the course. They will learn a lot more about God's attributes. What attitudes should they have as they face the remaining units? Don't rush their answers; let them get beyond the first superficial responses. The point of learning about God is to get to know Him better, to have a closer relationship with Him, and ultimately to become more like Him. Their attitudes—humility, trust, assurance, dependence, hope, and so on—will greatly determine whether the course is only an academic study or a life-changing experience.

Day 5
Enrichment Activities

1. Display two Scripture passages: Isaiah 55:8–9 and Deuteronomy 29:29. Have students creatively present the core truths in these verses—using art, music, writing, drama, or other media. These projects may be done individually or in groups.

2. Have students review what they've learned about God's incomprehensibility and ineffability and add that information to Interact 2.1, God's Attributes.

3. Distribute **Blackline Master 9.2, Unit 9 Quiz**.

Let God Be GOD

10

GOD **Is Omniscient and Omnipresent**

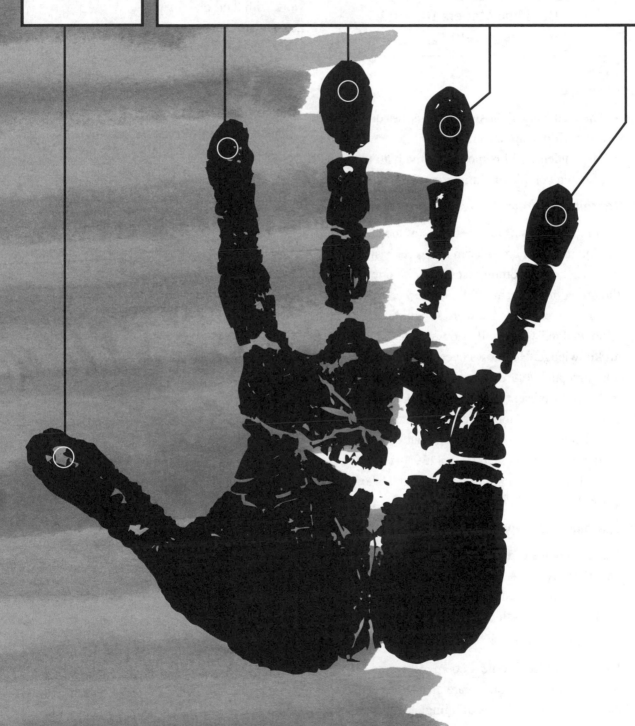

Unit 10 God Is Omniscient and Omnipresent

Memory Passage: Psalm 139:1–6

Lesson Materials:
    Blackline Masters 10.1–10.2
    Interacts 10.1–10.3

Day 1
Objectives

1. The students will answer and discuss questions about God's omniscience.
2. The students will respond creatively to the idea of being completely known by God.

Teaching Strategy 1

Remind students of the meanings of the attributes of God they will consider in this week's study: omniscience and omnipresence. Point out that the prefix *omni-* means "all"; *-science*, which has the same root as the word *science*, means "knowledge." God is all-knowing: that is, He has all knowledge. He knows everything, including all about me and you. God is also omnipresent: that is, He is all-present, or present everywhere. These two attributes of God are clearly related. Display **Blackline Master 10.1**, or write out Psalm 139:1 on the board. Then read Psalm 139:1–18 aloud, and ask students to point out places that show both attributes.

Teaching Strategy 2

Direct students to **Interact 10.1, God Is Omniscient**. Have them read and answer the questions individually or in small groups. Then lead a class discussion, using the answer key.

Teaching Strategy 3

Have the students write a poem (50 words or more), draw a cartoon, create an advertising slogan, or pen the lyrics of a jingle that relates to the fact that God knows everything about us. If they need ideas, suggest they reread their notes and the Scripture passages for Interact 10.1. Have students identify the biblical principle or passage they have in mind. Students who wish to do so may try more than one. In the last ten minutes, or in tomorrow's class, ask volunteers to share their work with their classmates.

Day 2
Objectives

1. The students will answer and discuss questions about God's omnipresence.
2. The students will construct a collage in which they present the attributes of God they've studied so far.

Teaching Strategy 1

Direct students to **Interact 10.2, God Is Omnipresent**. Have them answer the questions. Later, discuss Interact 10.2 with the students, using the answer key in this teacher guide for prompts and discussion starters.

Teaching Strategy 2

Divide the students into pairs or small groups. Have them scan the Interacts they've completed to review the attributes of God they've studied so far. Give each group a large sheet of construction paper and a stack of old magazines and newspapers to use for pictures and words, and have each pair make a collage about God's attributes. Each collage must have at least four pictures or other visual images and at least four words, phrases, or sentences. Be sure to display the finished collages.

Day 3
Objectives

1. The students will role-play a person whose "god" is a modern idol such as another person or a sport.
2. The students will evaluate each false god, challenging its adequacy as an object of worship.

Teaching Strategy 1

Ahead of time, write the name of each "god" listed below on a separate slip of paper, adding others that seem appropriate for your group. Put the slips into a basket or hat.

• my abilities
• academic achievement
• my car
• my friends
• money
• my social status at school
• my body
• great clothes
• my athletic ability
• my musical talent
• television
• movies
• sports stars
• my favorite sport
• my friends
• my pastor
• my big brother or sister
• my digital gadgets
• my favorite music
• my family
• my favorite websites

Ask a volunteer to remind the class of the meaning of the word *idolatry*: the worship of a created thing rather than the Creator. Then have each student choose one slip of paper. Ask students not to look at their slips of paper until all have drawn one and heard all your instructions.

Explain that each slip of paper names something that is sometimes so important to a person that it becomes an idol, or god. Ask each student to role-play a person who worships that god, explaining why it's the best god and why it is worth believing in.

For example, the student who drew "my favorite sport" might begin: "My god is baseball. It allows me to vent my emotions. Also, whether I'm

playing baseball or just watching a game, I'm with people who are just like me, and when I'm with people, I don't worry about anything." A student who drew "television" might say, "With television, I have all sorts of great adventures and visit wonderful places through the story characters. Also, a good TV program is an excuse not to do homework."

After each student finishes his or her role-play, have the class evaluate the reasons for belief in each god. They might ask:

• Will your feelings about this god always stay the same?
• Does this god explain what happens after death?
• How will you cope with life when you are not with this god?
• What if something happens and this god is no longer available to you?
• Does this god meet all your needs—mental and spiritual as well as physical and social?
• If this god is a person, what if he or she lets you down?

Teaching Strategy 2

In summary, remind students that words reveal less than actions about what people really value. Ask them to think about how they spend their daily resources of time, energy, and money. This will be the topic of study tomorrow. You may ask students to complete as homework all but the third part of **Interact 10.3, The "Gods" of My Life**.

Day 4
Objectives

1. The students will take a personal inventory to evaluate how they spend their resources of time, energy, and money.
2. The students will complete a Scripture search on idolatry.

Teaching Strategy 1

Direct the students' attention to Interact 10.3. If this activity was not completed as homework, allow students time to do it now. Then ask volunteers to share what they learned from the exercise.

What gods did students identify? Let them share items that took the most time, energy, and money. Try to have a productive discussion rather than simply focusing on personal revelations. Point out that different gods require different resources. For example, students may spend a lot of time on television but little money or energy.

Teaching Strategy 2

Explain that an item listed as a priority isn't necessarily an idol. However, it's good to check our priorities, motives, and values frequently because God hates idolatry. Ask students to review **Interact 3.4, The Dangers of Idolatry**, to refresh their memory about this important topic.

Teaching Strategy 3

Direct students to return to the final section of Interact 10.3. What personal response will they make to their evaluation of priorities?

Remind students that they've been thinking about how they spend their time, energy, and money. What has this told them about their "gods"? Where does God fit into the list? Are they happy with the priorities they've set for themselves? If not, now is a good time to make changes. You might ask volunteers to share one change that they intend to make.

Day 5
Enrichment Activities

1. Have students make a concordance study of the words *naked*, *nakedness*, and *covering* in Scripture. Suggest they choose verses that highlight different aspects of nakedness and covering. Genesis 2:25 says, "The man and his wife were both naked, and they felt no shame." Before the Fall, relationships were honest, open, and transparent, and people shared their vulnerabilities. Genesis 3:7 says, "Then the eyes of both of them were opened, and they realized they were naked; so they sewed fig leaves together and made coverings for themselves." Ever since, our response to scrutiny is to hide, cover up, shift blame, and avoid responsibility. See Isaiah 61:10, Psalm 32:1, and Psalm 91:4.

2. Some students might want to reflect on what they have learned about God's omniscience and omnipresence by writing a short story on fear, embarrassment, openness, honesty, or confrontation.

3. Ask students to write letters of reminder to themselves based on changes they decided to make in their priorities and in their use of resources (see day 4, teaching strategy 1). Provide envelopes. Have students enclose their letters, write their own address on the envelopes, and seal them. Collect the letters and save them for several months, or until next year, and then mail them back to the students.

4. Have students review what they've learned about God's omniscience and omnipresence and add that information to Interact 2.1, God's Attributes.

5. Distribute **Blackline Master 10.2, Unit 10 Quiz**.

Let God Be GOD

11 GOD Is Omnipotent

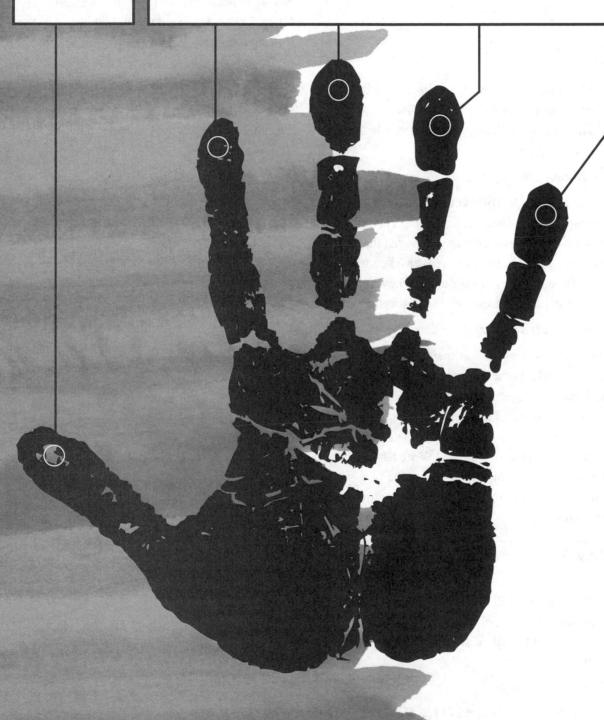

Let God Be GOD

Unit 11 God Is Omnipotent

Memory Passage: Colossians 1:16–20

Lesson Materials:
Blackline Masters 11.1–11.2
Interacts 11.1–11.4

Day 1
Objectives

1. The students will read and discuss Scripture passages that describe God's power.
2. The students will suggest responses to God in light of His power.

Teaching Strategy 1

Direct students to **Interact 11.1, God Is Omnipotent**, in their student book. Have them look up each reference and write what that reference says about God's power. Then lead a discussion, referring to the answer key in this teacher guide for questions and discussion starters.

Teaching Strategy 2

Have students review the answers they wrote on Interact 11.1. Ask a volunteer to read one of the Scripture passages; then ask several students to share their answers with the class. Then ask all the students, "How should we respond to the God who has this type of power?" Write responses on the board or on a flipchart. Repeat the process with other Scripture passages from the Interact as time allows.

Day 2
Objectives

1. The students will answer and discuss questions about God's unlimited creative power.
2. The students will personalize the implications of God's power.

Teaching Strategy 1

Direct students to **Interact 11.2, God's Creative Power**, in the student book and ask them to read and answer the questions independently. After

twenty minutes, discuss the answers as a class, referring to the answer key in this teacher guide for answers and prompts.

Teaching Strategy 2

Ask students to review what they wrote on Interact 11.2. Ask them to think about what those truths mean to them and what difference those truths should make in the way they think, speak, and act. Give students at least five minutes of silence in which to read and reflect. Then ask for volunteers to share their thoughts with the class.

Day 3
Objectives

1. The students will study the miracles of Jesus as examples of His omnipotence.
2. The students will personalize the implications of Jesus' power.

Teaching Strategy 1

Divide the class into groups of two to four students. Direct them to **Interact 11.3, Miracles of Jesus**, in the student book. Each group can work on the entire chart or on an assigned section of it. Either way, students can finish filling in their charts during the class discussion to follow.

Teaching Strategy 2

Ask students so-what questions related to each kind of power exhibited by Jesus. Use the answer key in this teacher guide as you lead a class discussion about Jesus' miracles.

Day 4
Objectives

1. The students will answer questions comparing God's omnipotence and human power.
2. The students will act out a situation in which they try to exercise their own power over others.
3. The students will discuss appropriate responses to God in light of His attributes, including omnipotence.

Teaching Strategy 1

Direct students to **Interact 11.4, God's Power and Ours**, in the student book. Have them work in groups of two or three to answer the questions. Afterward, ask the groups to share their answers with the class. Use the answer key to lead a discussion of the issues raised by these questions.

Teaching Strategy 2

Have the class brainstorm situations in which someone manipulates, intimidates, coerces, or acquires (MICA) in order to exercise power over someone else. You can entitle the activity, "I Have My MICA Degree."

Allow small groups to choose a situation to act out for the class. Have them develop a short skit, pantomime, or monologue. At the end of each group's performance, one member should explain briefly how the situation relates to God's omnipotence.

Read a story or recount a personal experience that illustrates deep devotion, wholehearted gratitude, or a loving response to another person. You might ask one or two volunteers to do the same.

Teaching Strategy 3

Review the attributes of God that your students have studied. They can refer to the entries they have made in Blackline Master 2.1, God's Attributes. Ask: Given God's nature, what should our response be? Have a volunteer read Deuteronomy 6 aloud. Then ask the following questions:

1. What commands did God give the people in this chapter? (Look for imperative verbs.)

2. What is the key verse for this chapter?

   Deuteronomy 6:5, "Love the Lord your God with all your heart, with all your soul, and with all your strength."

3. Why is the word *all* repeated in that verse? What are some synonyms for *all*?

   There is nothing half-hearted here! Some synonyms for all are *100 percent*, *complete*, *total*, *whole*, *every*.

4. What do other Scripture passages say about loving God? Look up Mark 12:28–34. What does Jesus call this command?

   The first or most important commandment.

5. How can we show our love toward God?

   By loving people. How we act toward others demonstrates what we believe.

Day 5
Enrichment Activities

1. Have a "Talk Back" day when students can discuss any issue, concern, or topic of their choice. Encourage students to refer to or apply biblical principles they have learned.

2. Display **Blackline Master 11.1, God's Power Questions**, and distribute copies to the students. Have students read Job 38–41, noting every question God asked Job. God's questions are meant to highlight the fact that God is God and Job isn't. The questions require Job to compare his power with God's. Have students create their own list of questions that God might ask us. Student questions should have the same purpose as God's questions to Job: to emphasize God's power.

3. Assign students to groups to study hymns related to God's omnipotence; for example, "All Hail the Power of Jesus' Name." They can research the hymn writer's background, the circumstance that inspired the hymn (if it is known), and the theme or message. Finally, they can make an illustrated poster about each hymn to display in the classroom or hallway.

4. Have students review what they've learned about God's omnipotence and add that information to Interact 2.1, God's Attributes.

5. Distribute **Blackline Master 11.2, Unit 11 Quiz**.

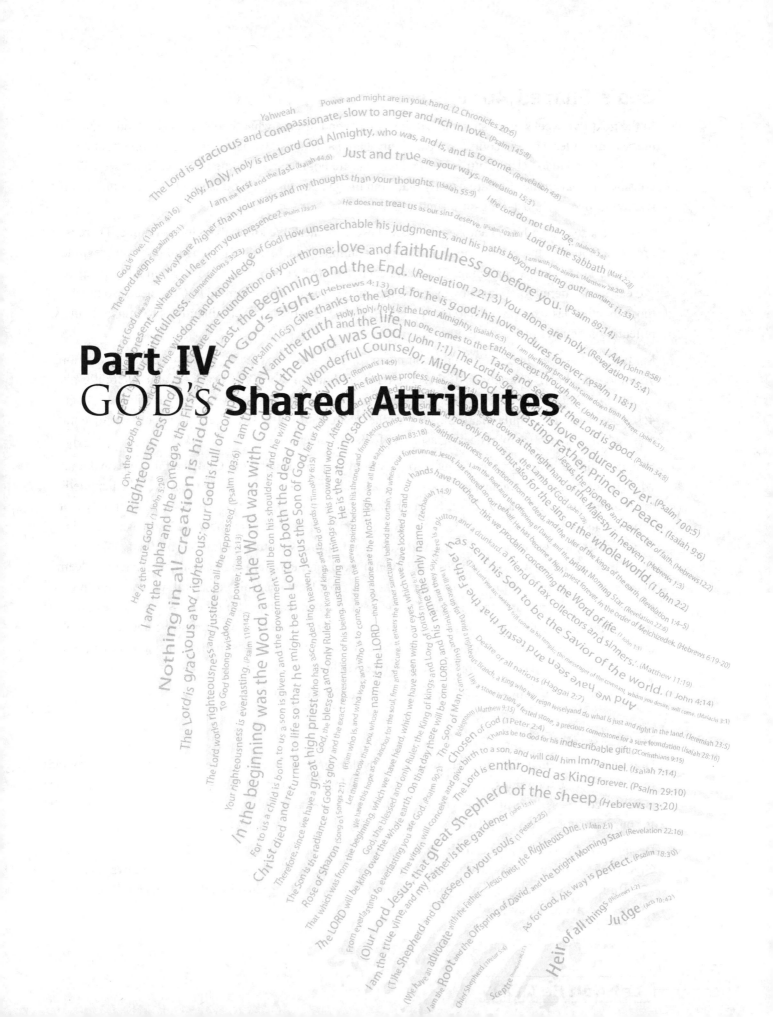

Part IV
GOD's Shared Attributes

God's Shared Attributes

In the next five weeks, your students will investigate and discuss what theologians call God's communicable attributes. (In this course, we call them shared attributes.) Christian thinkers throughout history have identified many shared attributes, and the lists are not identical. In the next five units, we will consider nine attributes that are usually placed in the shared column: God is good, wise, truthful, holy, righteous, merciful, just, long-suffering, and loving.

In what sense can both God and people share these attributes? We know that God is unique. There is only one God, and the gap between God and us is infinite (Isaiah 55:8–9). He is infinite; we are finite. He is eternal; we had a beginning. The world cannot contain Him; neither can any human language. We can show mercy to others; however, the meaning of *mercy* when applied to God means so much more than it does when applied to us. Nevertheless, in His Word, God commands us to imitate Him by reflecting a number of His attributes.

Many Christians are familiar with the command found in Leviticus 19:2: "Be holy because I, the Lord your God, am holy." (Variations of this command are found in Leviticus 11:44–45 and 20:26; it is also quoted in 1 Peter 1:16.) The apostle John said that because God is love, we should live in love (1 John 4:16). We will see a similar pattern with the other shared attributes. If we belong to God, we are commanded to imitate Him by reflecting aspects of His character.

Because human language is inadequate to fully communicate truth about God, we must use analogies when describing Him. An analogy does not mean that the meaning is exactly the same when applied to God and to us. An analogy describes a similarity between two things, but they are similar only in a certain sense—not in every way. For example, 1 John 3:16 says, "This is how we know what love is: Jesus Christ laid down his life for us. And we ought to lay down our lives for our brothers." We can never love the exact way Jesus loves. And even if we die for another person, our death cannot redeem that person from sin and make him or her a child of God. However, this verse still has some meaning if we ask, In what sense are we to imitate God by laying down our lives for others? We could describe our love using terms such as *unselfish*, *compassionate*, *giving*, *free*, and so on—terms we could also apply to God's love for us. So even though we can't be God, we can imitate Him enough so that other people can see that God is the model for our actions (see Matthew 5:16).

Following are brief summaries of the units that focus on God's shared attributes:

God Is Good

God does good things for His creatures. He holds the universe together, gives and sustains life, provides food and other good things, and freely bestows blessings. The attribute that produces these good actions is called goodness. This attribute gives God the right to define good and evil. He is the ultimate standard for our behavior. Everything He does is intrinsically good, and whatever He approves of is good.

Because God is good and because we are His, we are commanded to live in a way that is approved by God. If we identify ourselves as children of God, what we do directs honor or dishonor toward Him. The Bible contains many specific guidelines that help us identify behaviors that reflect God's goodness and help us avoid behaviors that don't.

God Is Wise and Truthful

God's wisdom is revealed in His work of creation. His laws, decrees, and plans also demonstrate wisdom. We share this attribute when we depend on God for wisdom (James 1:5) and when we exhibit other aspects of God's character in the way we exercise that wisdom.

God's Word is truth (John 17:17), and Jesus called Himself the truth (John 14:6). God's Word is absolutely reliable; He will do what He said He will do (Isaiah 55:10–11). We are to reflect this attribute not only by telling the truth but also by living lives of honesty, integrity, and transparency before others.

God Is Holy and Righteous

The attribute of holiness speaks of God's absolute uniqueness and His separateness from anything that isn't God. He is very different from any created thing. One of the implications of this separateness is that He is not subject to sin—something that cannot be said of the created world. We reflect this attribute by becoming different from the world and by not sinning.

Righteousness is related somewhat to goodness. God always does what is right, and He establishes the standard of right and wrong. Because God is righteous, He is qualified to be the ultimate judge; in fact, He is called the righteous judge (2 Timothy 4:8). He has the right to punish sin. He also has the right to remedy sin in other ways. His most astounding remedy for sin was to give His only Son to bear the punishment we deserve. We share in God's righteousness when we seek to be agents of His righteousness in the world. Throughout history, Christians have been at the forefront of efforts to alleviate human suffering—whether from sickness, slavery, oppression, or poverty.

God Is Merciful and Just

It is a fact that God does not treat us as we deserve. When we sin, He does not destroy us. Instead, He shows us mercy. We reflect this attribute when we show mercy and forgiveness toward those who have wronged us.

God supports the suffering and the exploited, and He will someday bring justice to the whole earth. We reflect God's justice when we care for those who are suffering injustice and when we work to reverse injustice and its effects.

God Is Long–Suffering and Loving

The word *long-suffering* means "patience" or "perseverance," but the word contains a metaphor that implies much more. God doesn't just work according to a different timetable. He doesn't just wait. While He is waiting for His will to be accomplished, He feels empathy and sympathy for His suffering people.

When John made the bold statement that God is love, he wasn't just supplying another attribute of God. He was describing what God is like in the core of His being. God defines what love is, and everything He does is motivated by love. Even His judgment on unbelievers is motivated by love within the Trinity and by His love for justice and holiness.

Romans 8:29 says, "For those God foreknew he also predestined to be conformed to the likeness of his Son, that he might be the firstborn among many brothers." What does it mean to be conformed to the likeness of Christ? There are many answers to that question, and the actions that are motivated by that goal will undergo some modification as you and your students grow in Christ. A study of God's communicable attributes can be a critical factor in the process of spiritual growth. If the goal is to be more like Christ, we need to understand better what Christ is like. Therefore, each of these lessons contains a strong application emphasis. Our goal is not only that our students will learn about God, but that they will become—as much as is possible for a human being—more conformed to God's character.

12 GOD **Is Good**

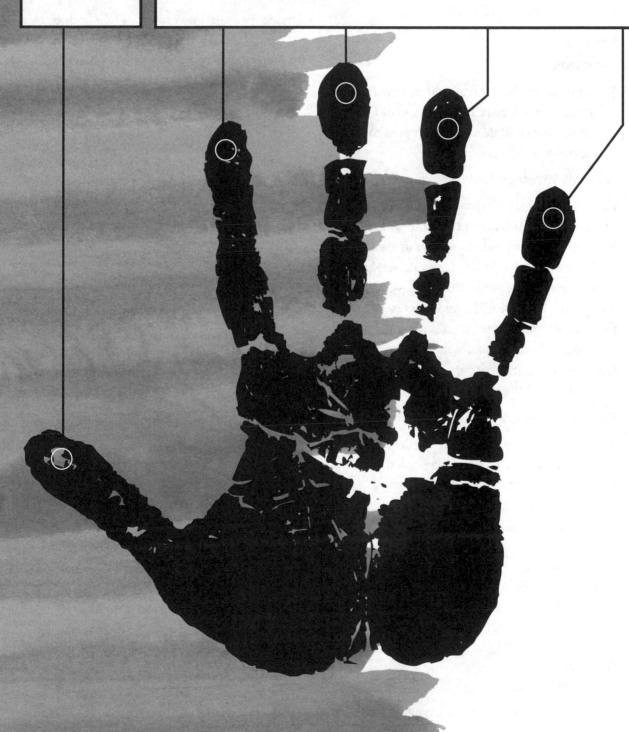

Unit 12 God Is Good

Memory Passage: Psalm 100:4–5

Lesson Materials:
  Blackline Masters 12.1–12.2
  Interacts 12.1–12.4

Day 1
Objectives

1. The students will look up and discuss Bible passages that declare the goodness of God.
2. The students will describe appropriate ways to respond to God's goodness.

Teaching Strategy 1

Have students look up the verses and answer the first question in **Interact 12.1, God Is Good**. Students may work individually or in small groups. When students have finished the Interact, have them share their answers with the class. Use the answer key in this teacher guide for discussion prompts. As you lead the discussion, call attention to the other divine attributes that are linked to God's goodness in these passages (or in the context).

Teaching Strategy 2

Ask students to suggest answers to the second question in Interact 12.1. If God is good, how should we respond to Him? Help students see that our responses can take the form of thoughts, attitudes, words, and actions. The purpose of this exercise is to reinforce the truth that our goal in learning about God's attributes isn't merely knowledge for its own sake. We want students to know God, not just know about Him; and knowing God should cause profound personal change.

Day 2
Objectives

1. The students will examine Scripture passages and summarize the ways in which God cares for His creation.

2. The students will share their findings with other students.
3. The students will plan appropriate ways to respond to God's benevolence.

Teaching Strategy 1

Divide the class into groups of two or three students. Have students turn to **Interact 12.2, God Is Benevolent**. Assign one of the passages to each group. (It is fine if several groups are studying the same passage.) Each group will read a passage and discuss what it says about God's benevolence. Then they will work together to write a paragraph summarizing their findings. When all groups have finished, have a student from each group read the paragraph to the class.

Teaching Strategy 2

Choose one of the passages listed on Interact 12.2. Lead a whole-class discussion on what that passage teaches about God's benevolence. Write those findings on the board. Then ask students to discuss, in groups of two or three, how they should respond to God's benevolence. Encourage them to suggest attitudes, actions, words, works of art, and other responses. You may wish to assign one of the other passages as homework.

Day 3
Objectives

1. The students will review what they've learned about God's goodness.
2. The students will explain how a belief in God's goodness can make a difference in their attitudes and actions.

Teaching Strategy 1

Display **Blackline Master 12.1, Is God Good?** or write "Is God Good?" across the top of the board. Divide the board down the middle. Write "Yes" at the top of one half. Lead students in a review of Interacts 12.1 and 12.2. As students talk about how God displays His goodness and how we should respond to that attribute, jot notes on that

Let God Be GOD

half of the board. When the student contributions are winding down—or when you've filled that half of the board!—write "Other Views" at the top of the other half. Ask students to share opinions they've heard that disagree with what was written on the first half. Ask them to think about opinions they might get from books, movies, songs, video games, conversations, and other sources. Lead students in a discussion comparing these viewpoints. Then ask, "What difference does it make to believe that God is good?

Teaching Strategy 2

Have students open their books to **Interact 12.3, Does God's Goodness Matter?** This Interact presents several facts; for each fact there are two responses. Divide the class into pairs. Assign one of the facts to each pair. One student will take one response; the other student will take the other response. Give the pairs a set amount of time to think about their assigned responses and figure out how to defend that response. When time is up, ask for volunteer pairs to come to the front and present the reasons for their responses. Students can present two short monologues, or they can conduct a back-and-forth discussion. When several pairs have given their presentations, ask the whole class, "What difference does it make to believe that God is good?" Ask them to go beyond the question of whether the statement "God is good" is true. Encourage them to answer the so-what question. The answer key in this teacher guide can help provide comments.

Day 4
Objectives

1. The students will read Bible passages teaching that they are to do good because God is good.
2. The students will discuss what would happen if Christians pursued good and avoided evil.
3. The students will set personal standards of conduct based on God's goodness.

Teaching Strategy 1

Have students turn to **Interact 12.4, Reflecting God's Goodness**. Students may work either individually or in pairs. When they have looked up the Scripture references and filled in the chart, ask for volunteers to share their answers with the class.

Teaching Strategy 2

Lead a discussion of why it is important for Christians to do good. Consult the answer key as needed. Have students review their answers on Interact 12.4 as they formulate their thoughts. Write their observations on the board. As you guide the discussion, help students understand that good works aren't a means to an end; they don't make God love us more, and they don't always make things better for us. We don't do such things so that people will think we're good people. We do good works to show that we belong to God, who is good. By doing such things, we reflect His character. We also show our commitment to Him by obeying His commands. The focus is on God and bringing glory to Him.

Day 5
Enrichment Activities

1. Expand the activity in teaching strategy 2, day 3. Divide the class into groups, and have each group choose one of the facts on Interact 12.3. Have students creatively illustrate each of the two statements explaining that fact. They can find images or articles in magazines, capture excerpts from movies or TV programs, write poems or advertisements, stage dramas or skits, or film original video presentations.

2. Have students review what they've learned about God's goodness and add that information to Interact 2.1, God's Attributes.

3. Distribute **Blackline Master 12.2, Unit 12 Quiz**.

13 | GOD Is Wise and Truthful

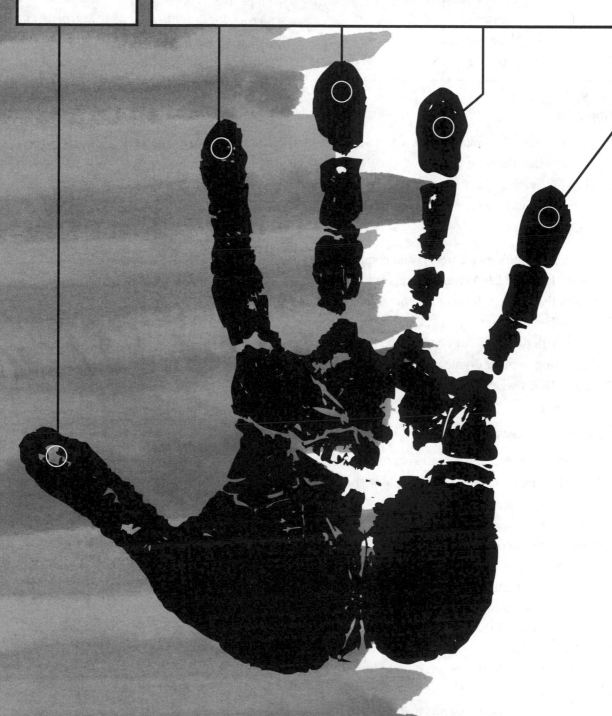

Unit 13 God Is Wise and Truthful

Memory Passages:

Job 12:13, Psalm 104:24

Lesson Materials:

Blackline Masters 13.1–13.3

Interacts 13.1–13.6

Day 1
Objectives

1. The students will look up and discuss Scripture passages that describe God as wise.
2. The students will describe appropriate ways to respond to God's wisdom.

Teaching Strategy 1

Have students look up the verses and complete **Interact 13.1, God Is Wise**. Students may work individually or in small groups. When students have finished the Interact, have them share their answers with the class. As you lead the discussion, call attention to other divine attributes that are linked to God's wisdom in these passages (or in the context).

Teaching Strategy 2

Ask students to review their answers to Interact 13.1. Ask, "If God is infinitely wise, how should that fact affect the way we think and act?" Help students see that our responses to God's wisdom can take the form of thoughts, attitudes, words, and actions. Perhaps the time when this issue comes to our attention is when we are confronted with one of God's commands for us. Is God wise enough to know all the implications of what He has told us to do? The purpose of this exercise is to reinforce the truth that our goal in learning about God's attributes isn't merely knowledge for its own sake. We want students to know God, not just know about Him; and knowing God should cause profound personal change.

Day 2
Objectives

1. The students will look up and discuss Scripture passages about how God shares His wisdom with people.
2. The students will identify areas of life in which they need wisdom from God.
3. The students will offer suggestions about how to acquire wisdom from God.

Teaching Strategy 1

Have students turn to **Interact 13.2, God's Wisdom for Us**. Students may work individually or in small groups. When students have finished the Interact, have them share their answers with the class. As you lead the discussion, help students identify broad areas of life in which God's wisdom is needed. Also call attention to passages that spell out specific ways of acquiring God's wisdom.

Teaching Strategy 2

Have students meet in groups of two or three. Ask each group to accumulate a list of situations they have personally faced in which God's wisdom was needed. These examples may take several forms: those in which people acted in God's wisdom, those in which people acted in their own wisdom, or those in which people's actions showed no evidence of wisdom. Give students a specified length of time for this activity. When the time is up, ask each group to share one example with the class. If you have time, ask groups for a second example. Ask the class what they can learn from these examples.

Day 3
Objectives

1. The students will study a chapter in Proverbs and analyze what the chapter says about wisdom.
2. The students will draw up personal plans for developing wisdom in their lives.

Teaching Strategy 1

Divide the class into groups of two or three. Have students turn to **Interact 13.3, Becoming Wise**. Assign each group one of the chapters from Proverbs indicated on the Interact: 1, 2, 3, 4, 8, or 9. Suggest that students have additional writing paper available. As students are reading, discussing, and writing, circulate around the room, giving advice and suggestions as needed.

When students have finished working on Interact 13.3, ask the groups to report their answers, in chapter order. Everyone who worked on chapter 1 will report on that chapter, then those who worked on chapter 2, and so on. Encourage the other students to take notes during these reports.

Teaching Strategy 2

After students have worked on Interact 13.3, have them turn to **Interact 13.4, My Wisdom Plan**. Ask them to work individually on a plan for acquiring God's wisdom. If time is short, assign it as homework. At the beginning of next class, students will report on their wisdom plans.

Day 4
Objectives

1. The students will share their personal wisdom plans with other students.
2. The students will look up and discuss Scripture passages that describe God as truthful.
3. The students will describe appropriate ways to respond to God's truthfulness.

Teaching Strategy 1

Divide the class into pairs. Have students turn to Interact 13.4. Have students share and compare their wisdom plans. Ask them to discuss why they wrote what they did. Encourage students to add to their own plans after this discussion if they wish.

Teaching Strategy 2

Introduce this activity by pointing out that the Bible speaks of God's truthfulness in two ways.

First, truth or truthfulness is an attribute that refers to God's character. God is trustworthy; He is not deceptive. The second meaning displays the first: His words, commands, laws, and other forms of communication are true. Because God is truthful, what He says is true. Have students complete **Interact 13.5, God Is Truthful**. Students may work individually or in small groups. When students have finished the Interact, have them share their answers with the class. As you lead the discussion, call attention to other divine attributes that are linked to God's truthfulness in these passages (or in the context). Also bring out the fact that because God is truthful, we can trust His written Word—the Bible.

Teaching Strategy 3

Just as with the other shared attributes, God's truthfulness places some requirements on us as His followers. Have students turn to **Interact 13.6, Reflecting God's Truthfulness**. Students may work individually or in small groups. When students have finished the Interact, lead a discussion on what it means to be people of truth. Help students see that the Bible is talking about an entire lifestyle of truthfulness. Truthfulness applies not only to our words, but also to our honesty, integrity, and trustworthiness.

Day 5
Enrichment Activities

1. Display **Blackline Master 13.1, Wisdom Matters**. Give students a few minutes to study and comment on the drawing. Divide the class into small groups. Have each group design and create a poster with the caption "Wisdom Matters." They may use art supplies to create their own graphic images, or they may cut out pictures and headlines from magazines and newspapers that illustrate the caption.

2. Display **Blackline Master 13.2, God Says**, and have students duplicate the format of

the blackline master on sheets of butcher paper or on a chalkboard. Divide the class into groups, and have each group specify a fact found in Scripture and a competing message from society. To give this activity the maximum impact, have students focus on moral imperatives. (The Ten Commandments would be a good starting place!) After identifying a scriptural imperative, have students look for specific messages from popular culture that disagree with God's command. (This project could be assigned as homework; the students would come to class prepared to share their answers.) The bottom-line question, of course, is, If God is truthful, who will we believe?

3. Have students review what they've learned about God's wisdom and truthfulness and add that information to Interact 2.1, God's Attributes.

4. Distribute **Blackline Master 13.3, Unit 13 Quiz**.

Let God Be GOD

14 GOD Is Holy and Righteous

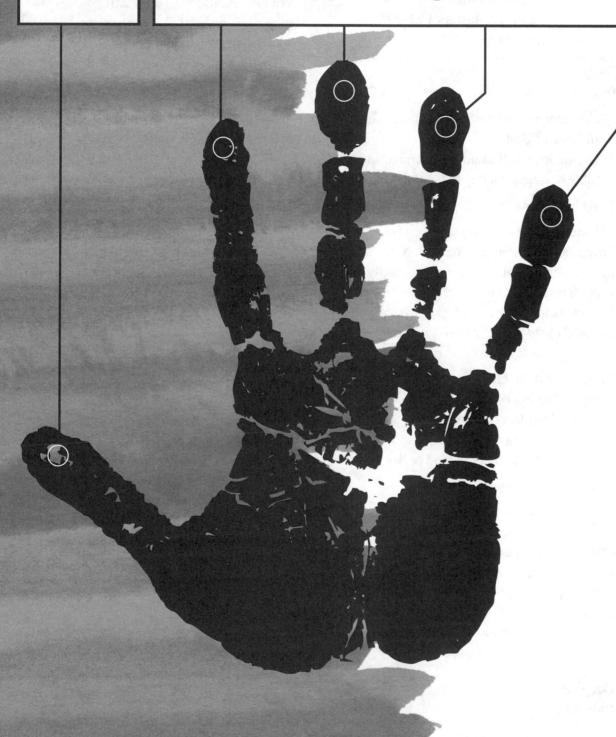

79

Unit 14 God Is Holy and Righteous

Memory Passage: Isaiah 6:1–7

Lesson Materials:
   Blackline Masters 14.1–14.2
   Interacts 14.1–14.2

Day 1
Objectives

1. The students will describe holiness as an attribute of God.
2. The students will examine, interpret, and apply Bible passages relating to God's holiness.

Teaching Strategy 1

Ask the students to define the word *holiness*. Encourage contributions from all. Note that most people identify holiness with moral purity or with high standards of conduct. You might ask volunteers to find the word *holy* in a dictionary and read aloud the definitions given. Bring out the following ideas:

As an attribute of God, holiness is the condition of being perfect in goodness. It also means "divine." As applied to places or objects, holiness is the condition of being set apart for a particular use, such as devoted entirely to God or His work.

Teaching Strategy 2

Have students turn to **Interact 14.1, God Is Holy**, in their student book. Assign to each student one of the six Bible passages on holiness. Students can work individually or in small groups as they write their answers. Explain that tomorrow in a class discussion they will share what they learned. You may wish to assign the remainder of the passages as homework.

Day 2
Objectives

1. The students will examine, interpret, and apply Bible passages relating to God's holiness.

2. The students will create a graffiti board defining and describing holiness.

Teaching Strategy 1

Lead the class in a discussion of the assignment from day 1, teaching strategy 2. If you assigned the Interact as homework, have the students take notes on a sheet of paper. For prompting and illustrations, refer to the answer key in this teacher guide.

Teaching Strategy 2

On a large sheet of butcher paper or on the chalkboard, have the students write graffiti. Title the paper or board "God's Holiness Is ..." Give the students time to complete the statement individually or in small groups. Display the graffiti as a reminder to the class of what God's holiness means and what it means to them.

Day 3
Objectives

1. The students will describe righteousness as an attribute of God.
2. The students will examine, interpret, and apply Bible passages relating to God's righteousness.

Teaching Strategy 1

Have students turn to **Interact 14.2, God Is Righteous,** in their student book. If you want to make this a graded assignment, have students work on a few of the references in class and then complete the Interact as homework. Students can work individually or in small groups as they write their answers. Explain that tomorrow in a class discussion they will share what they learned.

Teaching Strategy 2

Explain to the students that the Hebrew word translated "righteous" in the Old Testament referred to a person's status in relation to the law. One who kept the law or was found innocent in a court of law was called righteous. When applied to God (the lawgiver), the word referred to the rightness or appropriateness or justice of His laws. God is righteous because He determines what is right; His laws are consistent with His character. God is the righteous judge; He never makes a mistake in judging people. He is also the righteous ruler or king over His people and over all His creation. Call students' attention to the passages on Interact 14.2 that have to do with our falling short of God's righteous standard. When we compare ourselves to human law, we may look pretty good; but when we compare ourselves to God's righteous demands, we all fall short. That is why we must depend on Jesus' righteousness in order to be in right relationship with God.

Day 4
Objectives

1. The students will describe how it is possible for us to be holy.
2. The students will describe how it is possible for us to be righteous.

Teaching Strategy 1

Display **Blackline Master 14.1, Be Holy**, or write those verses on the board. Read the verses aloud. Divide the class into groups of no more than four students each. Have students review their notes on Interact 14.1. The students will answer the following question: "How can we reflect God's holiness?" Have one student in each group take notes and summarize the discussion.

Teaching Strategy 2

Divide the class into groups of no more than four students each. Have students review their notes on Interact 14.2. The students will answer the following question: "How can we reflect God's righteousness?" Have one student in each group take notes and summarize the discussion.

Day 5
Enrichment Activities

1. Using Bible dictionaries, encyclopedias, and other Bible study aids, the students can research the word *sanctification* (sanctify, sanctity). They will discover that in Greek this word comes from the same root as *holiness*. Have them notice when sanctification takes place (in the past, at our salvation; in the present, in our daily walk; and in the future, when Christ returns). They can further develop the topic by asking the Who? What? Where? Why? and How? questions about sanctification.

2. Have students review what they've learned about God's holiness and righteousness and add that information to Interact 2.1, God's Attributes.

3. Distribute **Blackline Master 14.2, Unit 14 Quiz**.

15 GOD Is Merciful and Just

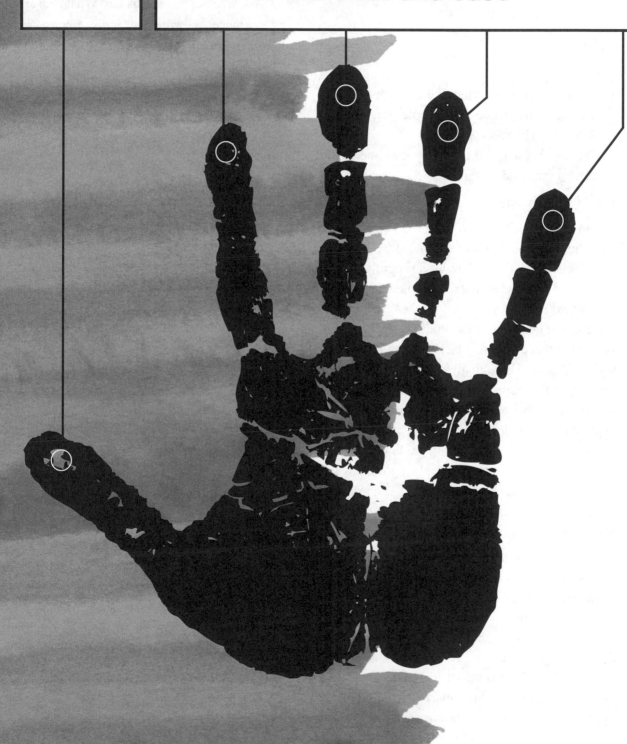

Unit 15 God Is Merciful and Just

Memory Passage: Psalm 103:8–12

Lesson Materials:
  Blackline Master 15.1
  Interacts 15.1–15.3

Day 1
Objectives

1. The students will review the concepts of mercy and justice as they role-play a classroom situation.
2. The students will gather data on the concept of mercy in the Old Testament.

Teaching Strategy 1

Ahead of time, ask for two volunteers to role-play a teacher and a student in a conflict situation: The teacher asks the student for a paper that is due today. The student hasn't completed it. The student explains why, and the teacher grants an extension. The next day the student asks for an additional grace period, which is given once again—this time grudgingly—by the teacher. Finally, on the student's third attempt to obtain an extension, the teacher demands the paper, explaining that failure to produce it by the day's end will result in a failing grade for the assignment. At this point the student goes into a tirade about the teacher's unfairness. The teacher motions the student out of the room. The student is still arguing on the way out the door.

After the class sees the role-play, point out that it demonstrated both mercy and justice. Write this definition of mercy on the board: "compassion that forbears punishing even when justice demands it." Ask how the teacher showed mercy. Then write this definition of justice: "fairness; conformity to a standard." Ask what the standard was in the role-play (the due date for the paper). Some students might point out that if the teacher had continued to be "merciful," the teacher would have been unjust to the students who met the deadline. Some might

think the teacher was already too "merciful." Issues of justice and mercy aren't always easy.

Direct the students to Proverbs 29:1. Ask whether this seems fair. Direct students back to Proverbs 28:13. Ask whether this seems fair. What choices do people make, and what are God's responses? Is God's judgment fair? This is our topic for the week.

Teaching Strategy 2

Write the word *immutable* on the chalkboard, and ask a volunteer to recall what we mean when we say that God is immutable. (You may want to refer them to unit 8.) Has God changed from Old Testament times to New Testament times? (No, He is the same eternally.) Ask a volunteer to read Numbers 23:19. Comment that many people, including Christians, have thought God was judgmental and angry in the Old Testament but merciful and loving in the New Testament. But God's attributes remain constant. His mercy and his justice are unfailing, consistent, balanced, and infinite. Explain that because of the common misconceptions about what God is like in the Old and New Testaments, we will look now at some Old Testament examples of God's mercy; later in the week we'll look at some New Testament examples of His justice.

Teaching Strategy 3

Direct the students to **Interact 15.1, Old Testament Mercy**, in their student book. Have them read the Scripture passages. They may answer the questions individually or in small groups, or you could guide them through the Interact as a whole class. For suggested responses, see the answer key in this teacher guide.

Day 2
Objectives

1. The students will look up Bible passages describing God's justice or mercy.

2. The students will discuss responses to God's justice and mercy.

Teaching Strategy 1

For this exercise, divide the class into groups of no more than four students. Give each group a Bible study tool that can be used to find references to God's justice and mercy. Some possible study resources are concordances, study Bibles, Bible dictionaries, Bible encyclopedias, Bible handbooks, and theology books. Give students a time limit for collecting references to God's justice and mercy. Have one member of the group act as recorder to list Scripture references and summarize the message of each reference. Ask the recorders to read the summaries to the class. Note the main points on the board.

Teaching Strategy 2

How should we respond to God's justice and mercy? Collect ideas from as many students as possible. Some responses will be individual, some corporate. They could include thanking God for His justice and mercy, singing songs that celebrate these attributes of God, practicing justice and mercy, helping those who have suffered injustice, working for just laws, and so on.

Day 3
Objectives

1. The students will read Isaiah 58 and 59 closely to answer questions about justice and mercy.
2. The students will consider the questions, God has been merciful to me, so how should I treat others? What can I do for others now?

Teaching Strategy 1

Direct the students to **Interact 15.2, Justice and Mercy**. Have them read the Scripture passages and answer the questions. After they have completed the Interact, discuss the answers as a class, using the answer key as needed.

Teaching Strategy 2

Isaiah 58 and 59 picture a time when many people had departed from God, justice seemed absent, and the need for mercy—including God's ultimate expression of mercy in Christ the Redeemer (59:20)—had never been clearer. Chapter 58 describes a number of ways God wanted His people to extend mercy to others (verses 6–14), and these are just as relevant today. With the whole class, discuss the following:

1. What is mercy?

   Besides the definition you put on the board on Day 1, mercy is a caring response to the miserable, hurting, and needy—to those who cannot help themselves.

2. Read Jeremiah 22:3, 15–16, and ask, Does this passage apply today? To whom should we show mercy?

   Especially mention people that students can actually help now, such as the elderly, poor, and ill in their own families and neighborhoods.

3. How should we show mercy? What are specific, personal, and measurable things we can do? How can we show our love for God by helping people?

   Review some of the specific ways of showing a caring response (including those in Isaiah 58:6–14). Besides individuals that can be helped, mention local charitable and other organizations that the class could become involved with.

Day 4
Objectives

1. The students will read Jesus' teachings about justice found in the book of Matthew.
2. The students will recognize that inequities in this life will be reconciled in the next life.
3. The students will consider the question, Why doesn't God punish evil and evildoers now?

Teaching Strategy 1

Direct the students to **Interact 15.3, New Testament Justice**, in their student book. Point out that in the New Testament, Jesus often spoke about justice, judgment, and hell. Jesus, who embodied the Father's grace and His undeserved mercy, will sit in judgment on those who reject God's compassion. Have students work individually or in small groups on the Bible passages listed. For ideas and prompts, refer to the answer key in this teacher guide.

Afterward, talk about what these Scriptures teach regarding Jesus' view of justice. Discuss the question, Why doesn't God punish evil and evildoers now?

The students can write notes from the discussion on the bottom portion of the Interact if they did not complete it as homework.

Teaching Strategy 2

Ask students to suggest four or five basic questions related to God's mercy and justice. These should be general. Write their suggestions on the board and use them to create a survey form. Have each student copy the questions, or make one master and distribute copies to the class. Each student should interview another student, a person at church, a neighbor, or a family member and record the answers. The results will serve as a basis for discussion tomorrow.

Teaching Strategy 3

Have selected students read the following passages and prepare a one-minute summary of what that passage says about God's mercy in salvation. Each person chooses a passage and has five minutes to prepare and one minute to present a summary.

Ephesians 2:4–5	Hebrews 4:15–16
1 Timothy 1:16–17	1 Peter 1:3
Titus 3:5	1 Peter 2:9–10

Day 5

Enrichment Activities

1. Have students debrief their experiences with the survey they developed in teaching strategy 2 on day 4. What did they learn about the way different people feel about the subject of God's mercy and justice? Were the answers of church people different from those who don't go to church? What answers surprised them? How would they answer some of the unbiblical answers they received?

2. Watch television programs or movies that highlight issues of justice. Report your observations to the class.

3. Have the students write a 250-word essay titled, "How Can God Be Just and Merciful at the Same Time?" Encourage the students to include biblical principles and to apply them personally and specifically. This can be done individually or as small-group projects.

4. Have the class skim Proverbs, looking for any references to mercy or justice. A few examples include 17:23, 18:5, 19:28, 21:15, 24:23–25, and 28:5. Have students draw political cartoons or comic strips to illustrate justice and mercy in the Scriptures.

5. Lead students in a short study of Romans 3:21–26. In light of what we've studied about God's justice and mercy, how can God be both "just" and "the one who justifies" people (verse 26)?

6. Have students review what they've learned about God's justice and mercy and add that information to Interact 2.1, God's Attributes.

7. Distribute **Blackline Master 15.1, Unit 15 Quiz**.

Let God Be GOD

16 GOD Is Long–Suffering and Loving

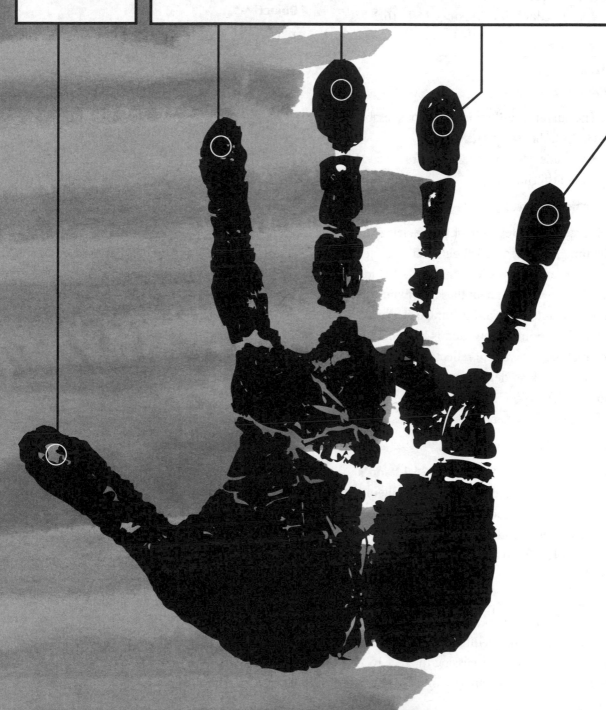

Unit 16 God Is Long–Suffering and Loving

Memory Passage: 2 Peter 3:8–9

Lesson Materials:
Blackline Masters 16.1–16.2
Interacts 16.1–16.4

Day 1
Objectives

1. The students will review previous lessons on God's holiness and justice.
2. The students will link God's wrath and His long-suffering.

Teaching Strategy 1

Give students a few minutes to review some of the things they learned about God's holiness (unit 14) and His justice (unit 15). As students recall information about these attributes, jot their findings on the board. Encourage students to move beyond describing how God is holy and just and mention how we are to reflect those attributes in our lives. Ask students to reflect on what is on the board. Then ask, How does God respond to people who violate His standards of holiness and justice?

Teaching Strategy 2

Direct the students to **Interact 16.1, God's Wrath**, in their student book. Have them complete the Interact individually or with partners. Then lead them in discussing God's wrath, referring to the answer key in this teacher guide.

The idea of God's wrath can be a difficult one for students, so it is important to bring out that God's anger or vengeance is different from human anger or vengeance. After discussing Interact 16.1, conclude by establishing the following differences.

The wrath of God is . . .
• not personal but judicial.
• not emotional but volitional.

• not vindictive but promised.
• not bitter but righteous.

God does not carry a grudge, but He acts as a judge.

Day 2
Objectives

1. The students will record biblical statements about God's long-suffering.
2. The students will apply God's long-suffering to real-life situations.

Teaching Strategy 1

Direct the students to **Interact 16.2, God's Long-Suffering**, in their student book. Have them follow the directions to complete the Interact. You may want to divide the class into small groups and give each group part 1, 2, or 3. Students should complete part 4 individually. Later, discuss God's long-suffering as students refer to their notes. Prompts and ideas are given in the answer key in the back of this teacher guide.

Teaching Strategy 2

Display **Blackline Master 16.1**. Read and discuss the quotation on the BLM. Then ask questions such as these: Who is speaking, and to whom? (One thief on the cross is speaking to the other thief about Jesus.) Is he right in what he says? What did he say next? How did Jesus respond, and what attribute of God do Jesus' words show? How are the thief's words relevant to us today?

Day 3
Objectives

1. The students will look up Scripture passages relating to God's love.
2. The students will link God's love to some of His other attributes.

Teaching Strategy 1

Have students look up the verses and answer the first question in **Interact 16.3, God Is Love**. Students may work individually or in small groups.

You may also wish to assign a portion of the Interact to each group. When students have finished the Interact, have them share their answers with the class. As you lead the discussion, call attention to the other divine attributes that are linked to God's love in these passages (or in the context).

Teaching Strategy 2

Ask students to suggest answers to the second question in Interact 16.3. If God is love, how should we respond to Him? Help students see that our responses can take the form of thoughts, attitudes, words, and actions. The purpose of this exercise is to reinforce the truth that our goal in learning about God's attributes isn't merely knowledge for its own sake. We want students to know God, not just know about Him; and knowing God should cause profound personal change.

Day 4
Objectives

1. The students will read passages from the book of Psalms that respond to God's love.
2. The students will create their own responses to God's love.

Teaching Strategy 1

Have students look up the verses and answer the questions in **Interact 16.4, Singing God's Love**. Students may work individually or in small groups. You may also wish to assign a portion of the verses to each group. When students have finished the Interact, have them share their answers with the class. As you lead the discussion, call attention to the effect that God's love has on the life of each psalm writer. The key question—for the psalm writers and for us—is, How can we live in God's love?

Teaching Strategy 2

Have students meet individually or in small groups to create their own responses to God's love. They could write lyrics that fit a familiar tune, compose a poem, draw a picture, develop a

PowerPoint presentation, make a video—whatever fits their inclinations and gifts. Students can present their creations tomorrow.

Day 5
Enrichment Activities

1. Have students display, perform, or present their creative projects from teaching strategy 2 on day 4.

2. With this unit, students have studied all the divine attributes covered in the course. Have a "Talk Back" session in which students can discuss any issue, concern, or topic of their choice related to the attributes of God. Encourage them to identify ways in which they can personally apply what they've learned.

3. Have students review what they've learned about God's long-suffering and love and add that information to Interact 2.1, God's Attributes.

4. Distribute **Blackline Master 16.2, Unit 16 Quiz**.

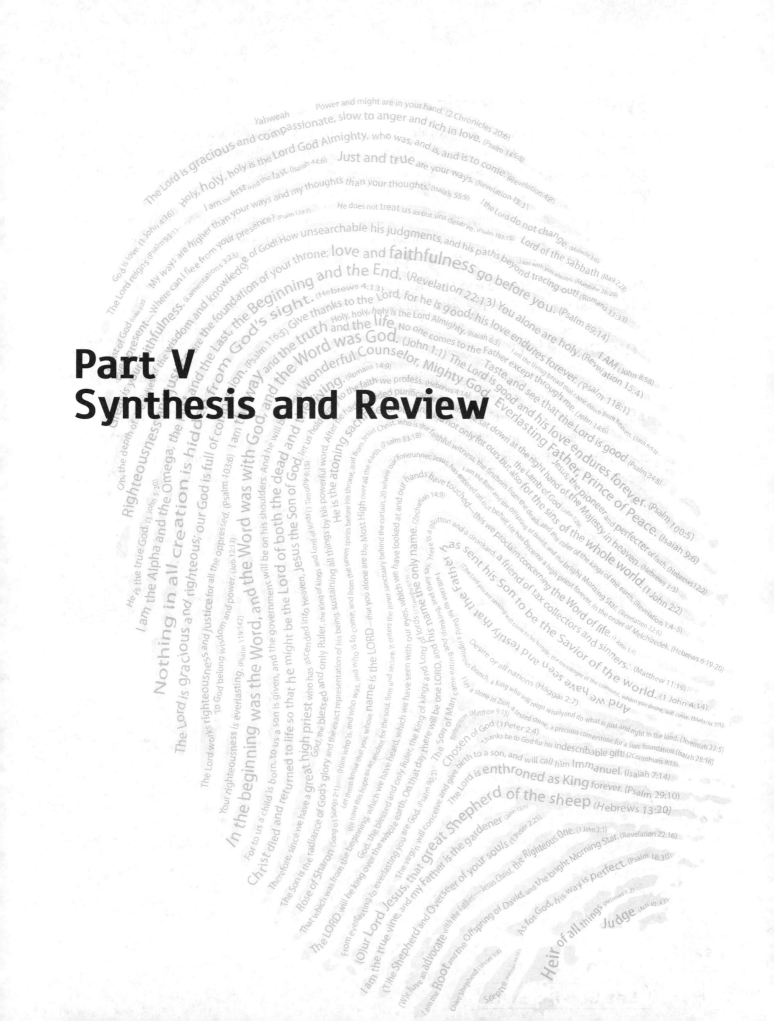

Part V
Synthesis and Review

Synthesis and Review

The final two units of the course provide an opportunity for your students to review the attributes they have studied and to reflect on the implications of those attributes. Because some attributes seem to contradict each other—or at least seem to work at cross-purposes—your students will benefit from activities that encourage a synthesis of the material they have studied.

In Unit 17, students will study, research, and discuss attributes that at first glance may seem to contradict each other. The activities in this unit will not only help students address specific pairs of attributes but will also equip them with a template for dealing with future questions about God's attributes.

Unit 18 provides structured review activities that will remind students of the specific attributes they have studied in the course. The week will end with a final exam and a course evaluation.

Teacher Alert

You will want to begin planning your final exam as soon as possible. Because the course was designed to allow a great deal of flexibility in content and emphasis, only you can identify the specific issues your students have dealt with this semester. Select items from the quizzes, Interacts, and blackline masters to create a final exam that reflects the subjects you have covered and emphasized. For example, you could reproduce Blackline Master 2.1 and give students one sheet as part of the exam; students would be required to complete all boxes in the chart for three attributes. You could also ask for short essays on selected attributes and topics.

17

GOD'S ATTRIBUTES:
Complementary or Contradictory?

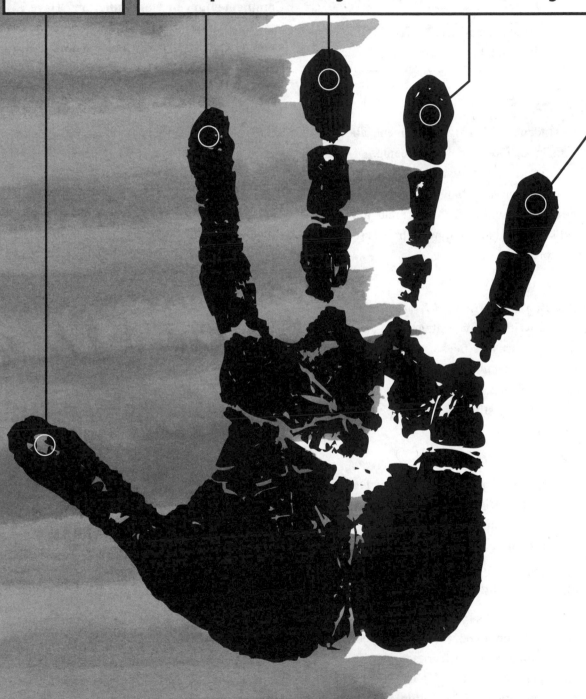

Unit 17 God's Attributes: Complementary or Contradictory?

Memory Passage: Revelation 15:1–4

Lesson Materials:
Blackline Masters 17.1–17.3
Interact 17.1

Day 1
Objectives

1. The students will analyze statements about God's love, agreeing or disagreeing.
2. The students will draw a diagram to represent complementary attributes of God.
3. The students will interpret Scripture about God's love and hate and will apply scriptural principles to their own lives.

Teaching Strategy 1

Display **Blackline Master 17.1, What Do You Think?** or write the five statements on the board or on a flip chart. Ask the students to read these to themselves, deciding whether they agree or disagree with each statement. Then discuss each statement, asking students to give specific reasons for their opinions.

Teaching Strategy 2

Emphasize the balance in God's character. Remind the students that His emotions and responses are not exactly like ours. Write the following sentence on the board, underscoring the italicized words:

"We must be careful not to identify *our* human emotions with *God's* perfect, balanced character."

Explain that if God's love is emphasized but His hate is never mentioned, for instance, people may never understand or fear that sin will bring eternal separation from God. Display the diagram on **Blackline Master 17.2, Complementary Attributes**, and have the students draw it on a sheet of paper and keep it in their notebook.

Explain that they should be careful to put opposite each other those attributes of God that appear to be contradictory.

Teaching Strategy 3

Direct the students to **Interact 17.1, Complementary or Contradictory?** Have them look up the verses that describe what and whom God loves or hates (the first section). From these verses they should be able to complete the first section. You may have students share their answers in class, or you can have them finish this Interact as homework.

Day 2
Objectives

1. The students will discuss personal applications regarding God's love and hate.
2. The students will identify other things that God loves and hates.

Teaching Strategy 1

If Interact 17.1 was assigned as homework, have students take notes on a separate sheet of paper. If the Interact was an in-class exercise, give a few minutes for students to complete the rest of the Interact.

Lead students through a discussion of their answers to the first section of the Interact. Then lead them through the remaining sections. Have a student read aloud each Bible passage referenced in the second section, and ask another student to suggest an answer. Then give all students a few minutes to write a summary in the third section.

Ask these follow-up questions. Suggested answers are provided to help stimulate discussion.
- Is love based on emotion or decision? (Decision.)
- How is love shown? (Through action.)
- Is fear part of a right response to God? (Yes. Fear includes trembling in God's presence and approaching Him with respect, reverence, and awe.)

• Is it easy to be a believer? (No, not for a person who reads, believes, and follows Scripture.)

• What did you learn about love and hate that you didn't know before? (Answers will vary.)

Teaching Strategy 2

Encourage students to continue the biblical search for things loved and things hated, either in class or as homework. You might suggest that they write these, with references, on happy and sad faces cut from construction paper. Placing the cutouts around the perimeter of a bulletin board will prepare it for additions tomorrow.

Day 3
Objectives

1. The students will look up and discuss verses relating to other complementary attributes of God.
2. The students will plan ways to explain pairs of complementary attributes.

Teaching Strategy 1

Divide the class into groups of no more than four students each. Display Blackline Master 17.2 and have the students take out the charts they made on day 1. Each group will choose one of the complementary pairs of attributes and begin to look for Bible passages that deal with each of the two attributes. (Note: If they are using concordances for their search, they will want to look up synonyms also.) Following the pattern in the first section of Interact 17.1, students are to list the references and write a descriptive sentence or phrase for each verse.

Teaching Strategy 2

Have each group of students plan a way to present the complementary attributes they have chosen. They may communicate it in writing, visual arts, music, or using other media. They should be prepared to give their presentation at the beginning of tomorrow's class.

Day 4
Objectives

1. The students will present their complementary-attributes projects.
2. The students will review some of the main features of the course.
3. The students will express the importance of knowing God.

Teaching Strategy 1

Give students a chance to present the projects they worked on yesterday. A representative from each group should give some background related to the project. Then the whole group will present the project.

Teaching Strategy 2

Have students turn to the table of contents in their student book and read over the topics they have studied in this course. Give them a few minutes to flip through the books and skim any notes they have taken. Then lead the class in a big-picture discussion of the course. The following questions may stimulate some discussion:

• What new things did you learn about God?

• What familiar things about God do you now understand more fully than before?

• How has this course deepened your relationship with God?

• How has it affected your relationships with other Christians?

Students will no doubt bring up other issues. Close the class by reading Ephesians 1:17. Let the students know that this is your prayer for them: that they will continue to know God better.

Day 5
Enrichment Activities

1. Arrange for the students' projects to be displayed to other classes in the school. Perhaps some of them can be used in a chapel service.

Let God Be GOD

2. Suggest a reading list for students who wish to do an in-depth study of one of God's attributes.

3. Ask a pastor or youth leader to speak to students about their own spiritual growth. The guest should provide practical suggestions for getting to know God better.

4. Distribute **Blackline Master 17.3, Unit 17 Quiz**.

18 Course Review, Final Exam, and Evaluation

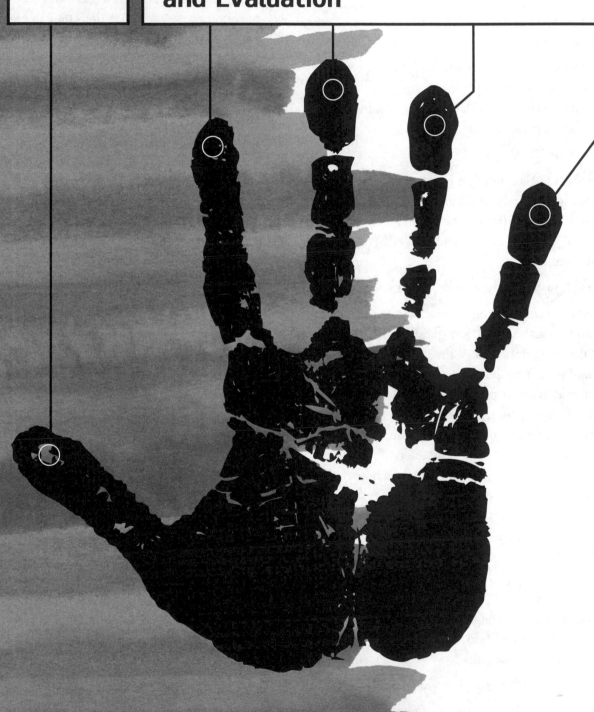

Unit 18 Course Review, Final Exam, and Evaluation

Lesson Materials:
Blackline Masters 18.1–18.2

Day 1
Objectives

1. The students will review the lesson content from units 1 through 4.
2. The students will ask questions about what they studied in those units.

Teaching Strategy 1

Divide the class into groups of two or three students. Have the students review the Interacts and the quizzes from units 1 through 4. They should jot down notes about items they want more information on.

Teaching Strategy 2

Bring the students together as a class. Ask those who took notes to ask any questions they thought of during their review. Write the questions on the board. When all the questions have been collected, you may want to group some of the related questions for efficiency. Briefly lead a discussion about each group of questions. Assure students that questions that go beyond the course content will not be on the final exam. Make a note of those questions so that you can recommend resources for those who want to pursue those issues.

Day 2
Objectives

1. The students will review the lesson content from units 5 through 11.
2. The students will ask questions about what they studied in those units.

Teaching Strategy 1

Divide the class into groups of two or three students. Have the students review the Interacts and the quizzes from units 5 through 11. They should jot down notes about items they want more information on. Have them update Interact 2.1 (Blackline Master 2.1) to make sure it is complete.

Teaching Strategy 2

Bring the students together as a class. Ask those who took notes to ask any questions they thought of during their review. Write the questions on the board. When all the questions have been collected, you may want to group some of the related questions for efficiency. Briefly lead a discussion about each group of questions. Assure students that questions that go beyond the course content will not be on the final exam. Make a note of those questions so that you can recommend resources for those who want to pursue those issues.

Day 3
Objectives

1. The students will review the lesson content from units 12 through 17.
2. The students will ask questions about what they studied in those units.

Teaching Strategy 1

Divide the class into groups of two or three students. Have the students review the Interacts and the quizzes from units 12 through 17. They should jot down notes about items they want more information on. Have them update Interact 2.1 (Blackline Master 2.1) to make sure it is complete.

Teaching Strategy 2

Bring the students together as a class. Ask those who took notes to ask any questions they thought of during their review. Write the questions on the board. When all the questions have been collected, you may want to group some of the related questions for efficiency. Briefly lead a discussion about each group of questions. Assure students that questions that go beyond the course content will not be on the final exam. Make a note of those questions so that you can recommend resources for those who want to pursue those issues.

Day 4
Objective

The students will take their final exam for the course.

Teaching Strategy 1

Select items from the quizzes, Interacts, and blackline masters to create the final exam for the course. For example, you could reproduce Blackline Master 2.1 and have students fill out the blank chart for three attributes. You could also ask for short essays on selected attributes and topics.

Teaching Strategy 2

Students who finish the final exam early may begin filling out a course evaluation.

Day 5
Enrichment Activities

1. Return students' final exams and provide feedback on them.

2. Use this final day for "Talk Back." Allow students to reflect on and discuss the course as a whole. What did they learn that they had not known before? What was most helpful? What additional materials or activities would they include for future students?

3. Distribute **Blackline Master 18.1, Course Evaluation**. Ask the students to evaluate the course more formally by completing the evaluation form.

4. Distribute **Blackline Master 18.2, Final Commitment**. Lead the students in a time of personal reflection and commitment. This must be voluntary. Do not have them submit any part of the answers. Do not require them to answer the commitment questions unless they want to. Give them as much time as they desire.

You may want students to keep this statement of commitment, or you may want to provide envelopes. Students can then seal their responses in the envelopes and address the envelopes to themselves. Explain that you will mail these back to students at the end of the following semester or school year.

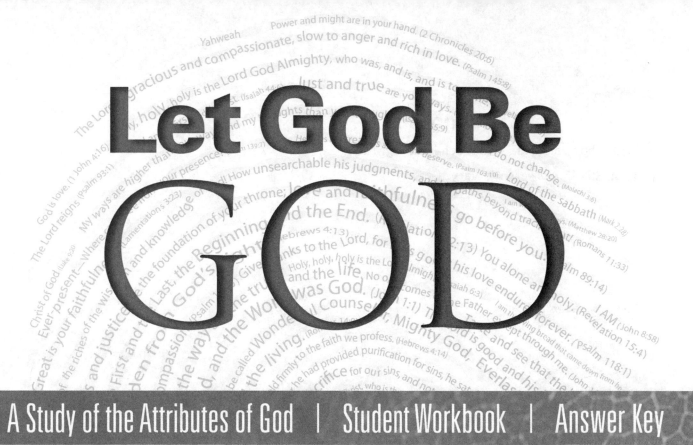

Let God Be GOD

A Study of the Attributes of God | Student Workbook | Answer Key

Mark Eckel

Interact 1.1
Labeling God

Write about the kind of God each label suggests.

Town Sheriff Answers will vary.

Store Manager

Santa Claus or Aladdin's Genie

Party Animal

Grandfather

God-in-a-Box

Let God Be GOD

Interact 1.2

Can We Define God?

Read Job 38–41, and answer these questions. **Answers will vary.**

1. What is the problem with treating God like one of the titles on Interact 1.1?

2. According to God, how does the Creator compare with the creature? Give three specific statements from Job 38–41 in which God compares himself with Job.

Follow-up question to #2: Why is it important for us to have an accurate concept of God?

3. How is God's description of Himself in Job 38–41 different from popular ideas about God?

4. What happens to our view of God when we make up our own ideas about God?

Follow-up question to #4: Which idea of God is more satisfying to people—the one they come up with themselves or the one presented in the Bible?

5. Is it possible to define God? Give reasons for your answer.

6. How would you summarize, in one sentence, the message of Job 38–41?

Let God Be GOD

Interact 1.3

God Makes Himself Known

God has deliberately revealed Himself in ways that human beings can understand.

Definitions

Revelation is the disclosure of something previously unknown. Bible scholars divide the means of revelation into two categories:
- *general* or *unlimited revelation*—available to all people everywhere
- *specific* or *limited revelation*—available only to certain people at certain times

Research

Look up the references listed in the left-hand column to match them to the means of revelation listed on the right. (Some references will have two correct answers. Give both answers.)

Reference	Means
1. Exodus 10:1–2 **D**	A. Scripture
2. Numbers 12:6–8 **E** and **G**	B. Christ (the Incarnation)
3. Psalm 19:1, 7 **F** and **A**	C. conscience
4. John 1:1, 14, 18 **B**	D. history/miracles
5. Romans 2:14–15 **C**	E. face-to-face (theophany)
6. Colossians 1:15 **B**	F. nature
7. 2 Timothy 3:16 **A**	G. the prophets (including visions and dreams)
8. Hebrews 1:1–2 **G** and **B**	
9. 2 Peter 1:19–21 **A**	
10. Romans 1:20 **F**	

Which two means of revelation listed above are in the *general revelation* category?

Conscience and nature

What is our main source for special revelation?

Scripture

Let God Be GOD

Interact 1.4

The O–I–C–A Method

Examine Genesis 1:1 closely. Answer the questions for the O-I-C-A method of Bible study.

Answers will vary.

Observation: What does the verse say?

Interpretation: What did the verse mean *for the first readers, then*?

Correlation: How does the verse fit in with other Scripture?

Application: What does the verse mean for *us, now*?

O

I

C

A

Let God Be GOD

Interact 2.1
God's Attributes

You will be completing this chart throughout the course.

Attribute	Meaning	Symbol	Reference(s)
Supreme	God is the only God, above all "gods."		Isaiah 40:18, 25
Self-existent	God is not dependent on anything or anyone.		Answers will vary.
Sovereign	God has absolute authority.		Isaiah 40:10
Infinite	God is unlimited and perfect.		Answers will vary.
Immutable	God never changes.		Answers will vary.
Eternal	God always was, is, and will be.		Answers will vary.
Incomprehensible	We can't know God fully.		Answers will vary.
Ineffable	We can't adequately describe God.		Answers will vary.
Omniscient	God knows everything.		Answers will vary.
Omnipresent	God is fully present everywhere.		Answers will vary.

Continued on back →

Let God Be GOD

Attribute	Meaning	Symbol	Reference(s)
Omnipotent	God is all-powerful.		Answers will vary.
Good	God is good in all He does, and sets the standard for our goodness.		Answers will vary.
Wise	God is wise in His works, laws, and plans.		Answers will vary.
Truthful	God is truth and His Word is truth.		Answers will vary.
Holy	God is unique and sinless.		Answers will vary.
Righteous	God is the righteous judge, and sets the standard for righteousness.		Answers will vary.
Merciful	God does not treat us as we deserve.		Answers will vary.
Just	God supports victims of injustice and will someday bring perfect justice.		Answers will vary.
Long-Suffering	God patiently cares for His people.		Answers will vary.
Loving	God is love, and is motivated by love.		Answers will vary.

Let God Be GOD

Interact 2.2
God and People

Read Acts 17:22–31, and answer the first question.

1. What do these verses tell us about God and people?

God	People
Made the world and everything it it; Lord of heaven and earth; does not live in temples built by hands; does not need anything; distributed people over the earth; determined their times and places; cannot be represented by images made by people; one day He will judge the world by Jesus Christ.	**Created by God; dependent on God; under the rule of God; "in him we live and move and have our being" (verse 28); God's offspring.**

2. With knowledge comes responsibility, and Paul gave information about God to the people in Athens. According to Paul, what did God want the people to do with that knowledge?

   Reach out to Him and find Him; repent.

Let God Be GOD

Monotheism vs. Polytheism

Monotheism		Polytheism
Answers will vary.	**Definition**	Answers will vary.
	Religions	
	Divine names	
	Divine character	
	Believers' attitudes	
	Effect on believers' lives	
	"Advantages" of this belief	
	"Disadvantages" of this belief	
	So what?	

Let God Be GOD

Interact 3.2

God vs. "Gods" in Ancient Israel

Canaanite "gods"		God
1 Chronicles 16:26, Isaiah 44:15 Idols; created by people; can create nothing.	Creation	**Genesis 1:1** God created everything.
Amos 5:26 People made their own gods; these gods are not alive.	Eternity	**Psalm 90:2** God is eternal Spirit; He always was and always will be—"from everlasting to everlasting."
1 Kings 18:25–29 Baal was powerless.	Power	**1 Kings 18:30–39** God demonstrated His power.
Deuteronomy 4:28, Isaiah 44:9 These gods couldn't see, hear, or know.	Knowledge	**Psalm 19:14; 139:23** God is all-knowing; He knows our thoughts and motives better than we do.
1 Samuel 7:3 The Canaanites worshipped many gods.	Worship	**1 Samuel 7:3** The Israelites were commanded to worship the Lord their God only.
Isaiah 44:10 Idols were nothing; they could provide nothing for their worshippers.	Provision	**Psalm 50:15; 68:7–10; Deuteronomy 11:14–15** God provides abundantly for His people; He provides food, drink, and deliverance from enemies.
2 Kings 23:7 Canaanite worship involved immoral practices.	Morality	**Leviticus 11:44** God commands His people to be holy because He is holy.

Let God Be GOD

Idols and Idol Makers

God Challenges Idol Worshippers (Isaiah 44:6–8)

• What does God say about Himself?

He is Israel's King and Redeemer, the Lord Almighty, the first and the last, the only God.

• What challenge does He make to the readers of this chapter?

Foretell what will happen.

God's Opinion of Idol Makers (Isaiah 44:9–12)

• What does God say about those who make idols?

They are nothing; blind and ignorant.

• Why do you think God was so harsh?

Answers will vary.

Why Idols Are Silly (Isaiah 44:13–20)

• Why does an idol make no sense?

An idol maker uses part of the log for an idol and uses the rest for firewood.

• What is an idol—really?

Just a piece of wood.

• Why do people worship idols?

They have "a deluded heart" (verse 20).

111

Interact 3.4
The Dangers of Idolatry

Find and read each verse or passage of Scripture, and answer the questions.

1. Read Romans 1:21–24 and Psalm 4:2. What is idolatry?
Idolatry is worshipping something created rather than the Creator, ascribing a higher value to an object or person than to God, and expecting that object or person to be the source of happiness, satisfaction, and power.

2. Read Exodus 20:3 and Revelation 21:8 and 22:15. What is God's attitude toward idolatry?
He forbids it, hates it, and punishes it.

3. Idolatry has links to what other sins?

Colossians 3:5
Greed

1 Corinthians 6:9
Sexual immorality

Ephesians 5:5
Greed, immorality, impurity

Galatians 5:20
Witchcraft, hatred, selfish ambition

1 Corinthians 5:10
Immorality, greed, extortion

1 Samuel 15:23
Divination

4. Read 1 Corinthians 10:14. What is God's command concerning idolatry?
We are to flee it, to put it away.

Let God Be GOD

Interact 4.1
The Trinity

Look up each verse or passage and write what it tells you about one or more of the members of the Trinity—the Father, Son, and Holy Spirit. (Note: Sometimes the text says "God" instead of "Father.")

Matthew 3:16–17

All three persons were involved in Jesus' baptism.

Matthew 28:19

We are to baptize new believers in the name of all three persons.

John 16:12–15

The Father and the Son were involved in the sending of the Holy Spirit.

Acts 2:32–33

God raised Jesus and seated Him at the Father's right hand; Jesus poured out the Spirit on Pentecost.

Acts 11:15–17

God gave the Holy Spirit to those who believed in Jesus.

Acts 20:27–28

The apostle proclaimed the whole will of God; the Holy Spirit appointed elders; they are shepherds of the church of God; Jesus is God.

Romans 1:1–4

Paul was set apart for the gospel of God; the Holy Spirit spoke through the prophets; Jesus is the Son of God.

Romans 8:1–4

Believers are in Christ Jesus; we have the Spirit of life; God sent His Son to become a man and become a sin offering for us; we live according to the Spirit.

Let God Be GOD

1 Corinthians 12:3–6

The Holy Spirit enables us to say, "Jesus is Lord"; there are different gifts, but the same Spirit; different kinds of service, but the same Lord; different kinds of working, but the same God.

2 Corinthians 13:11, 14

To say that God is with us is to say that the Lord Jesus Christ, God, and the Holy Spirit are with us.

Ephesians 4:4–6

There is one Spirit, one Lord, and one God and Father of all.

2 Thessalonians 2:13–14

Paul thanks God for the Thessalonians, who are loved by the Lord and chosen to be saved through the sanctifying work of the Spirit.

Titus 3:4–7

All three persons are involved in our salvation.

1 Peter 1:2

Peter wrote to those who had been "chosen according to the foreknowledge of God the Father, through the sanctifying work of the Spirit, for obedience to Jesus Christ."

1 Peter 4:14

If you suffer because of Christ, the Spirit of glory and of God rests on you.

1 John 4:2–3

The Spirit of God acknowledges that Jesus Christ comes from God.

Interact 4.2

God the Father

In a concordance, find verses in the New Testament that contain the word *Father* or *God*. Write the references in the left-hand column. Look up each verse. Beside each reference, write an answer to the question in the right-hand column.

Verses about the Father	How do these verses show that the Father is God?
Answers will vary.	Answers will vary.

Let God Be GOD

Interact 4.3
God the Son

In a concordance, find verses in the New Testament that contain the word *Son* or *Jesus* or *Christ*. Write the references in the left-hand column. Look up each verse. Beside each reference, write an answer to the question in the right-hand column.

Verses about Jesus	How do these verses show that Jesus is God?
Answers will vary.	Answers will vary.

Let God Be GOD

Interact 4.4
God the Holy Spirit

In a concordance, find verses in the New Testament that contain the words **Holy Spirit** or **Spirit**. Write the references in the left-hand column. Look up each verse. Beside each reference, write an answer to the question in the right-hand column.

Verses about the Holy Spirit	How do these verses show that the Holy Spirit is God?
Answers will vary.	Answers will vary.

Let God Be GOD

Interact 5.1
God Is Supreme

1. The following Bible passages talk about the supremacy of God. As you read each passage, answer this question: Over what or whom is God supreme?

1 Chronicles 29:11–12

Heaven and earth

2 Chronicles 20:6

The kingdoms of the nations

Job 38:1–6

The earth

Psalm 8:1

The heavens

Psalm 19:1–2

Over the heavens and the skies

Psalm 24:1–2

The earth and all who live in it

Psalm 93:1

The world

Psalm 95:1–6

All gods, depths of the earth, mountain peaks, sea

Psalm 113:1–9

The earth, the nations, the heavens, poor and oppressed people

Psalm 145:3–7

Over all (implied)

Isaiah 40:25–26

Over all, the stars

Isaiah 42:8

Idols

Isaiah 44:6

Over all

Isaiah 45:22

The earth, over all

Isaiah 46:5

Over all

Isaiah 55:8–11

Over human thoughts, over the earth

Ephesians 1:20–21

Over all rule and authority, power and dominion, now and in the age to come

Philippians 2:9–11

Above every name in heaven, on the earth, and under the earth

Colossians 1:15–20

All creation, the church, rulers, everything in heaven and earth

Hebrews 1:1–4

All things, angels

Let God Be GOD

 **Interact 5.1 Continued**

Revelation 4:8–11

All things

Revelation 5:11–14

Over all

Revelation 7:9–12

Over all

Revelation 15:1–4

All nations

2. What other attributes do the writers link to God's supremacy?
Answers will vary.

3. According to these passages, how should we respond to the fact that God is supreme?
(You may have to look in the surrounding verses to find a response.)
Answers will vary; the main response is worship.

God's Supremacy Matters

Look up the following passages from Psalm 118. After reading each passage, answer the questions.

Psalm 118:5–7

• How did God show that He is supreme?

He answered the psalmist's cry for help.

• What difference did God's action make in the life of this psalmist?

God set him free, took away his fear.

Psalm 118:8–9

• What are some things we trust in?

Other people, princes.

• Why is it better to trust in the Lord?

Answers will vary.

Psalm 118:13–14

• How did God show that He is supreme?

He saved the psalmist.

• What difference did God's action make in the life of this psalmist?

He is the psalmist's strength and song.

Psalm 118:15–16

• What are some "mighty things" you have seen God do?

Answers will vary.

• How do you respond when God helps you?

Answers will vary.

Psalm 118:19–21

• Why is the psalmist thankful?

God saved him.

• What do you have to be thankful for?

Answers will vary.

Let God Be GOD

Psalm 118:22–24

• Who has rejected the Lord today?

Answers will vary.

• What reasons do we have for rejoicing anyway?

Answers will vary.

Psalm 118:25–27

• What New Testament event does this passage remind you of?

Jesus rides into Jerusalem on a donkey while people shout.

• Why do we have even more reasons to rejoice than this psalmist did?

Answers will vary. Since the coming of Christ, we know much more about God's works.

Psalm 118:28–29

• How can you show your thanks to God?

Answers will vary.

• How can you exalt Him in your life?

Answers will vary.

Interact 5.3
Before Genesis 1:1

Find and read each verse or passage of Scripture, and answer the questions. **Answers will vary.**

1. Describe what reality was like before Genesis 1:1. You may use words, artwork, symbols, or anything else that you think will help communicate what you want to say. Be prepared to explain your work.

2. Look up the following verses: Psalm 90:2, Psalm 93:2, Isaiah 40:28, and Acts 17:24–25. How do these verses add to your knowledge of God's self-existence?

Let God Be GOD

Interact 6.1

God Is Sovereign

Look up the following passages and jot down the main points about God's sovereignty in creation, in people's lives, and in events.

Genesis 50:20

God can turn people's evil deeds to His good purposes.

Exodus 8:15, 32; 9:7, 12, 34–35; 10:1–2, 20, 27; 11:9–10; 14:1–4, 8

God's purposes in delivering Israel are realized in the repeated hardening of Pharaoh's heart, so that all these events will bring glory to His name.

1 Kings 12:15

God appears to have caused the king not to listen to the people in order that God's word might be fulfilled.

Psalm 115:3

God is free to do whatever He pleases.

Psalm 139:16

David says that God knew him and determined the days of his life before he was born.

Proverbs 16:1, 4, 9, 33; 19:21

These proverbs say that even though we can plan what we think is right, the Lord determines the outcome.

Proverbs 21:30

Ideas that oppose God show neither wisdom nor understanding.

Isaiah 45:1–7

God chooses and uses Cyrus, even though he does not believe in God; God creates light and darkness, prosperity and disaster.

 Interact 6.1 Continued

Isaiah 46:9–11

What God plans will happen. He will do all that He pleases.

Lamentations 3:37–38

God is sovereign over good and evil.

Matthew 10:29–31

God is sovereign over every sparrow that falls and every hair on our heads.

Acts 2:22–23

God's predetermined plan was that Jesus would be crucified; His crucifixion was also the responsibility of humans.

Acts 17:24–31

God created because He wished to do so, not because He needed to. He determines where and when people will live.

Romans 8:28–39

Nothing is outside of God's rule; therefore, nothing can separate us from His love.

Ephesians 1:9–12

All things are accomplished to God's own good pleasure, which He ordained before time began.

Ephesians 2:4–10

God created us to do good works that God had prepared for us long before He saved us.

Interact 7.1
My Limitations

1. What things or forces limit your movements, your actions, your possibilities, and so on? List as many limitations as you can. The following questions might stimulate your thinking:

What keeps you from flying like Superman?

What keeps you from living in outer space or under the ocean?

What keeps you from knowing everything?

What keeps you from running at the speed of sound?

What keeps you from lifting a huge building?

What keeps you from bowling a perfect game every time? **Answers will vary.**

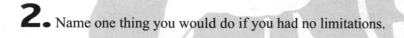

2. Name one thing you would do if you had no limitations.

125

Let God Be GOD

Interact 7.2
God Is Infinite

1. When we say that God is infinite, we are saying something about what He is *not*. Since *finite* means "having limits," to describe God as infinite is to say that He has no limits.

According to these verses, what are some of the ways in which God is not limited?

Deuteronomy 4:39   Above heaven and earth

1 Kings 8:27   Not limited by the highest heaven

Psalm 139:1–4   Unlimited knowledge

Isaiah 40:12–14   Unlimited mind; unlimited knowledge

Isaiah 40:25–26   Unlimited creative power

Isaiah 44:6–8   Unlimited by time

2. There is another meaning of *infinite*: "perfect." Something that is limited does not reach its potential. It falls short of what it could be. It is not perfect. But God is perfect in every way.

According to these verses, what are some of the ways in which God is perfect?

Exodus 33:19   Perfect mercy and compassion

Psalm 18:30–31   Perfect shield and refuge

Psalm 103:8   Perfect compassion, grace, patience, and love

Psalm 118:1   Perfect love

Isaiah 41:10   Perfect strength and righteousness

Let God Be GOD

Interact 7.3
God's Infinite Attributes

The following attributes are called God's "shared attributes" because we can use the same word to describe God and human beings. However, even though the word can be used for human beings, the meaning changes a lot when we use the word to describe God!

Choose an attribute from this list: *good*, *wise*, *truthful*, *holy*, *righteous*, *merciful*, *just*, *long-suffering*, or *loving*.

Attribute:_____ Answers will vary.

1. Give examples of things that *human beings* can do to show this attribute.

2. Give examples of things that *God* does to show this attribute. (Remember that God is infinite, so He has no limitations and does everything perfectly.) Give a Bible reference for every action of God that you mention.

Let God Be GOD

 Interact 8.1

God Is Immutable

Explore what it means for us that God is immutable, or unchanging.

1. Record what these verses tell us about God, along with your own thoughts and questions.

Numbers 23:19–20

God is immutable. He is not like a human person, who can change his or her mind. What He says He will do, He will do.

1 Samuel 15:29

God does not change His mind.

Psalm 110:4

What the Lord says, He will not go back on.

Isaiah 46:9–11

What God plans will take place; He does not change His plan.

Malachi 3:6

God's choice of Israel would never change.

Romans 2:1–11 (especially verse 11)

God judges according to truth. He is forbearing and long-suffering, and His goodness leads people to repentance. He never shows partiality.

2. Answer the following questions and explain how the fact that God is immutable bears on these issues:

• What are some fads you have witnessed?

• When does something become old-fashioned or outdated?

• Does the fact that something is new make it right, good, or best?

• Does being old make something wrong or inferior?

Fads are here for a short time and then they're gone. (Ask students to name some current fads.) Often fads are styles in clothes, foods, and music—short-lived, mutable, changeable. Sometimes we think something new is better than something old, and we call the old stuff old-fashioned. Biblical word old in Old Testament simply refers to time. Old Testament teachings about God's attributes, for example, are as relevant today as ever, because God does not change.

Let God Be GOD

 **Interact 8.1 Continued**

3. People cry for equality and consistency and justice. How does God's immutability affect these issues?

There must be one unchangeable source of truth, authority, and ethics. The immutable God is the only reliable foundation for justice, and He provides absolute standards for right and wrong.

4. Christians are supposed to reflect God's character. Select a characteristic from the list below, read the verse associated with it, and explain why it is especially important for Christians to show that characteristic.

Honesty. Proverbs 14:5

Trustworthiness. Titus 2:10

Sincerity. Romans 12:11

Integrity. Titus 2:7

Dependability. Proverbs 13:17

Good reputation. 3 John 12

Responsibility. Nehemiah 9:8

Truthfulness. Proverbs 12:22

Faithfulness. 1 Corinthians 4:2

Right intentions. Proverbs 14:22

Answers will vary.

Let God Be GOD

Interact 8.2

Can a Changeless God Change?

The verses listed in the chart below suggest that God may have changed His mind. Look up each passage, and in the first column describe the specific circumstances of God's actions. Then in the second column summarize how these verses might better be explained than by saying that God changed.

	Circumstances	God can't change, so …
Genesis 6:5–8	The people of Noah's day have sinned so greatly that judgment must fall.	God was grieved by the people; in His mercy, He gave them another 120 years to repent before the flood.
Exodus 32:9–14	God told Moses He would destroy the people because they were unfaithful; they turned from Him and worshipped a golden calf.	God doesn't change His mind; He fulfills His promises to Moses and the people.
Judges 2:17–18	God gave His people judges, but the people continued to be unfaithful; still, God delivered them from their enemies.	After a period of judgment, God has compassion on His people and sends a deliverer.
1 Samuel 15:1–11	Saul sinned against God by not fully obeying His commands.	God was grieved that He had made Saul king because of Saul's foolish choices.
Jeremiah 18:7–10	God gave a general command about judging those who disobey His laws and blessing those who obey.	God devised a plan that caused His people to repent, and He sent prophets to show His compassion.
Amos 7:1–6	In a vision the prophet Amos saw the judgment that God planned against Israel for their sin.	God sent prophets to warn His people.
Jonah 3:1–10	The people of Nineveh sinned greatly against God.	God sent Jonah to warn them to repent; they did, and God postponed His judgment.

Let God Be GOD

Interact 8.3
God Is Eternal

Explore what it means for us that God is eternal.

1. Discover what these Scriptures tell us about God. Write your answers below, along with your own thoughts and questions. Job 36:26; Psalm 90:2, 4; Isaiah 45:21, 46:9–10; 2 Peter 3:8

God is eternal and lives in eternity. God does not live in time as we know it; He created time. He is the only God and always was, is, and will be throughout eternity.

2. Consider two possibilities for what is eternal, or lasts forever. What difference does it make which you believe? MATTER IS ETERNAL or GOD IS ETERNAL

If God is eternal, He is in control. He sets standards of right and wrong, so we have a basis for our actions. If only matter is eternal, there is no personal Creator who sets standards and who gives eternal life.

3. Compare and contrast the following pairs of statements:

Good guys finish last.
The first shall be last and the last first.

The first statement seems to suggest that "bad guys," who are willing to do wrong, succeed. Jesus' words say that God will right the wrongs of this life; those who are now "first," or honored will be "last," or judged, in eternity.

Only the fittest survive.
He who loses his life shall save it.

The first idea, from the theory of evolution, means that the strong will save themselves. Jesus' words say much the opposite: one who sacrifices his life now will be saved in eternity.

It's a dog-eat-dog world.
If your enemy is hungry, feed him.

The first statement says that one must climb over others to get ahead or succeed. Jesus commands the opposite: we should help others, even our enemies.

4. How does the fact that God is eternal affect the statement pairs in question 3?

The first statement in each pair stresses this life over the next. If God were not eternal, that might be a reasonable choice. But God is eternal and the afterlife exists, so Jesus' words in the second statement in each pair are a better guide to life.

131

5. Explain why those who believe God is eternal have a stronger case for opposing rape, bigotry, murder, or any other deviant act.

If God were not eternal, His standards wouldn't be the ultimate authority for human behavior. People would live by human standards. No one could tell anyone else what to do. The standard for right and wrong would be left to the strongest. An absolute standard from the eternal God is more practical and sensible for real life.

6. When we sin, what happens if we repent? Does God remember our sins forever? Are they eternal too? See Psalm 103:11–12.

Scripture tells us that when we repent, God separates our sins as far as the east is from the west. This is an infinite distance since east and west have no poles (as do north and south). God removes our guilt forever.

7. If God no longer remembers our sins after He forgives us, why can't we forget them too? Why do wrong actions of our past sometimes haunt us?

We bear the scars of past actions. The results of our sin often remain evident (Leviticus 26:40–45, 1 Timothy 5:24–25). But Paul's example shows us that we should forget as part of God's forgiveness (Philippians 3:1–6, 14–15).

8. God is eternal, but we are temporal; we live in time, and time is limited. What are some tactics we can use to make better use of our time? See Psalm 39:4–6; Psalm 90:7–12; Ephesians 5:15–17; James 4:14–17.

Because time is limited, we need to use it well. Suggested tactics will vary.

9. An old song says that we should live "with eternity's values in view." What does this mean? How does each activity mentioned in Colossians 3:1–14 reflect "eternity's values"?

Answers will vary.

Let God Be GOD

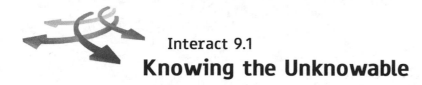

Interact 9.1
Knowing the Unknowable

1. Look up the following Bible passages and be prepared to discuss them:

Ephesians 1:17b–19

The Holy Spirit must open the eyes of our heart to enable us to know Him better, even though we can't know His "incomparably great power" completely.

Jeremiah 9:23–24

Knowing God is the most important thing.

John 17:3

To know God is life eternal.

Philippians 3:8

Knowing Jesus is the most important thing.

2. How should God's incomprehensibility affect the way we study the Bible?

We should be humble. Our knowledge will always be incomplete.

Interact 9.2
I Can Know God

My assigned psalms:_____ **Answers will vary.**

God's actions	God's character	Names or metaphors for God

Let God Be GOD

Interact 9.3
Picture a Person

Imagine a human being. Choose a characteristic for each of the categories in the list.

Age

Male or female

Height

Weight

Skin color

Hair color

Hair length

Glasses?

Other facial features

Clothes

Shoes

Income

Car model

Education level

Personality

Talents

Health issues

Moral standards

Religion

Hobbies

Habits

Marital status

Occupation

Family members

Friends

Let God Be GOD

Interact 9.4
Describing God's Love

The Bible often presents the same truth (or similar truths) in a variety of ways. The following passages all have something to say about God's love. Read each passage; then answer the question for that passage.

1. Statement. John 3:16, Romans 5:7–8, 1 John 4:16, 19.

What facts about God's love do you find in these passages?

God's love is unconditional; it is His nature.

2. Parable. Luke 15:11–32.

Jesus told this story. Many people see the father as God and the sons as His people. What can this story teach us about God's love?

Answers will vary.

3. Prophecy. Hosea 11:1–11.

In this prophecy, God talks to His people. What does this prophecy tell us about God's love for His people?

He continues to love them even though they have rejected Him.

4. Poetry. Psalm 103

In this poem, David sings about God's love for His people. What does this poem tell us about God's love? How does David want us to respond to God's love?

David uses many metaphors, including that of a compassionate father.

5. History. Exodus 16.

God can show His love in historical accounts, even if the word *love* isn't mentioned! How does this historical passage show God's love?

God continues to provide for His people, even when they are far from lovable!

Let God Be GOD

Interact 10.1
God Is Omniscient

Look up the Scripture verses and passages listed, and answer the questions. Feel free to write down any thoughts or questions you have as you work through this Interact.

1. Read Psalm 19:12–14, 1 Timothy 6:10–16, and Hebrews 4:12–13. What are some implications of God's knowing all our thoughts, motives, and intentions?

Students may use such words as fearful, scary, embarrassing, and so on. In Hebrews 4:12–13, the words "laid bare" originally conveyed the idea of a lamb with its neck bent back, exposing its throat just before the knife ends its life. Even today the word suggests complete exposure and vulnerability, without defenses.

2. Read Genesis 3:9–13 in its context. Why did God ask Adam and Eve four questions in the garden? Didn't He know the answers?

Consider other uses of questions in the Bible. (Jesus asked a lot of them!) Even today we use questions to produce self-examination, exposure, and heightened sense of responsibility. When Mom says, "Have you been eating cookies before dinner again?" she knows the answer. In Genesis 3 God asked Adam and Eve questions to "call them out," to confront them and give them an opportunity to repent. This shows God's mercy and grace. He wants people to accept responsibility and repent.

3. What about the time when God sent angels to see about the situation in Sodom and Gomorrah? Didn't He know? (See Genesis 18:20–21.) Remember, God is communicating with humans.

In this case, God shows His mercy, His "bending over backward" for people. By displaying His presence in Sodom, God shows that He will use extreme measures to bring people to Himself (2 Peter 3:9). Because God will judge humans, He sends angels in human form to communicate His concern. God's judgment does not come without ample warning or a lot of time.

4. Omniscience refers to knowledge. Brainstorm slogans, commercials, or other advertisements that use words such as *knowledge*, *brains*, or *school* to make a point. For example:

The more you know, the more you'll grow.

Be smart; stay in school.

Don't waste a good brain.

Answers will vary.

Interact 10.2

God Is Omnipresent

Answer the questions below. Add your own thoughts, insights, and examples.

1. List some of the ways in which we humans are limited by time and space.

Answers will vary.

2. What are some books, television shows, and movies that emphasize humanity's search for ways around time and space boundaries?

Answers will vary.

3. Why do people want to go beyond time and space limitations?

Answers will vary.

4. Read Psalm 139:1–12, Amos 9:2–4, Matthew 28:20, and Hebrews 13:5–6. List positive and negative aspects of God's omnipresence for humans.

Positive	Negative
God knows where I am.	I don't always go where I should
God hears everything I say.	I don't always say what I should.
God witnesses everything I do.	I don't always do what I should.
God is always with me.	I can't get away with anything.
God is always there when I need to ask Him for help.	I can't escape God.

Let God Be GOD

Interact 10.3

The "Gods" of My Life

Complete the following activities to find out about your personal "gods." **Answers will vary.**

1. Rank your expenditures of time, energy, and money for each item listed. Rank them from 0 (lowest) to 10 (highest).

Item	Time	Energy	Money
Technology and media (television, radio, video games, Internet, music, texting, etc.)			
School, homework, reading, studying			
Stuff—crafts, collections, other possessions			
Sports, exercise, hobbies			
Friends			
My looks (clothes, hair, etc.)			
Making money			
Personal time and space, thinking and dreaming			
Family relationships			
Relationship with God (prayer, Bible reading/study, devotions, church activities, etc.)			

2. This evaluation reveals the following about me:

3. I plan to make these changes:

Let God Be GOD

Interact 11.1

God Is Omnipotent

Look up each Bible passage and summarize what it says about God's power.

Job 26:7–14

God has power over everything in the universe.

Psalm 29:3–9

God has absolute power over every created thing, including seas and mountains and nations.

Psalm 68:32–35

His power is shown in the skies and in the temple.

Psalm 89:8–13

God has complete power over every created thing.

Jeremiah 10:12–13

God has complete power over every created thing.

Daniel 4:34–35

God has complete power over heaven and earth and all people.

Habakkuk 3:3–6

God has complete power over every created thing.

Let God Be GOD

Interact 11.2
God's Creative Power

Look up the Bible passages and answer the questions. Feel free to write your own thoughts as you meditate on what you discover. **Answers will vary.**

1. Read Psalm 96:4–6. What comparisons does the psalmist make between God and false gods?

2. Read Isaiah 40:12–17, 21–26. What does the natural world reveal about God? How does God compare with other sources of power?

3. Read Acts 17:24–28. How does God expect us to respond to His creative power?

4. Read 1 Corinthians 8:4–8. What are some false gods we encounter today? How should we respond to the attractions of false gods?

Let God Be GOD

Interact 11.3
Miracles of Jesus

Look up the Scripture passages and answer the questions. Notice how Jesus' miracles demonstrate God's omnipotence.

1. Skim the Gospel of Mark and complete the chart.

Reference	Miracle	God has power over ...
1:25	Demoniac healing	Satan, demons
1:31	Peter's mother-in-law healed	Illness
1:40–42	Leper healed	Incurable disease
2:5–12	Paralytic healed	Birth defects
3:5	Withered hand healed	Birth defects
4:39	Storm calmed	Physical world, weather
5:8	Demoniac healed	Satan, demons, personal distress
5:29	Bleeding stopped	Illness
5:41	Jairus' daughter raised	Death
6:41	Feeding of 5,000	Physical
6:48	Walking on the sea	Physical world
7:29	Demoniac girl healed	Satan, demons
7:34–35	Deaf man healed	Birth defects
8:6	Feeding of 4,000	Physical world
8:25	Blind man healed	Birth defects
9:25	Demoniac boy healed	Satan, demons
10:52	Blind man healed	Birth defects
11:7	Riding a wild colt	Animal world
11:14, 21	Cursing a fig tree	Physical world

2. Basing your answer on your study of Jesus' miracles, what are some areas in which Jesus showed God's power and authority?

Distress, personal turmoil, illness, injury, daily needs (food), Satanic oppression, the physical world, animals, death.

Let God Be GOD

 **Interact 11.3 Continued**

3. A miracle is something only God can do. In other words, God steps into the affairs of humans, sets aside the natural order He created, and does something supernatural. What were some effects of Jesus' miracles, other than physical effects?

More people believed; God was glorified; Jesus' message was validated; the people were amazed at Jesus' authority.

4. Can we command God to perform a miracle? (See 2 Corinthians 12:7–9.)

No; even Paul had to live with a "thorn" in his "flesh." The Lord told Paul: "My grace is sufficient for you, for my power is made perfect in weakness."

5. Does God ever perform a miracle today? If so, under what circumstances?

God still performs miracles today, but He does so in His own time to accomplish His purposes. The greatest miracle of all, however, is the transformation of a human being into a child of God.

Interact 11.4
God's Power and Ours

Answer the following questions. Feel free to add your own questions and ideas.

1. Can God do anything? Can God do everything? Explain.

No. God cannot contradict His own character. God cannot sin, for He is holy. He cannot change Himself or His plans, for He is immutable.

2. Can God create a rock so large He can't lift it?

God cannot build a rock so large He can't move it because God cannot stop being God. He must act consistently with His own nature, or attributes. It is in God's nature to have power over His creation. If God were limited by His creation, He would cease being God. (Of course, the question is purely hypothetical since the word *lift* makes sense only when talking about created things.)

3. The words *manipulation*, *intimidation*, *coercion*, and *acquisition* suggest ways in which humans sometimes try to exercise power. Look up any words you don't know, and find synonyms or related words. Think of a personal example for each, describing something you've done or something you've seen others do.

Manipulation suggests exploiting, using, orchestrating, controlling, managing, or handling.

Intimidation suggests using threats.

Coercion suggests exerting pressure, forcing, or compelling people.

Acquisition suggests getting, possessing, or gaining things.

Personal examples will vary.

4. How does our human desire for power relate to God's omnipotence?

We sometimes try to play God. We try to get our own way, usually for selfish motives.

Let God Be GOD

Interact 12.1
God Is Good

1. The following Bible passages talk about the goodness of God. As you read each passage, write *why* the author says God is good. (Look for actions of God that show He is good; also look for other attributes that the writers link to God's goodness.)

Genesis 18:25   God is the righteous Judge.

Deuteronomy 32:3–4   God does no wrong; His works are perfect; He is faithful.

1 Chronicles 16:34   God's love endures forever.

2 Chronicles 5:13, 7:3   God's love endures forever.

Ezra 3:10–11   God's love endures forever.

Psalm 25:4–10   God is loving, merciful, forgiving, and faithful; He guides and teaches; He is our hope.

Psalm 34:8   We can take refuge in Him.

Psalm 54:6–7   God's name is good; He delivers those who trust in Him.

Psalm 86:5   God is forgiving and loving.

Psalm 100:4–5   God is loving and faithful.

Psalm 106:1   God's love endures forever.

Psalm 107:1   God's love endures forever.

Psalm 116:1–7   God heard my cry for mercy and saved me; He is gracious and righteous; He protects me.

Let God Be GOD

Psalm 118:1, 29   God's love endures forever.

Psalm 119:68   What God does is good.

Psalm 135:3–4   The Lord is good to His people.

Psalm 136:1   God's love endures forever.

Nahum 1:7   The Lord is a refuge in times of trouble; He cares for His people.

Mark 10:18, Luke 18:19   Only God is good.

John 10:11–15   Jesus is the good shepherd who lays down His life for His sheep.

1 Peter 2:2–3   We have tasted that the Lord is good.

2. According to these passages, how should we respond to the fact that God is good? (You may have to look in the surrounding verses to find a response.)

Answers will vary. The usual response is worship and thanksgiving.

Interact 12.2
God Is Benevolent

In Matthew 5:45, Jesus describes God this way: "He causes his sun to rise on the evil and the good, and sends rain on the righteous and the unrighteous." Psalm 145:17 says, "The Lord is righteous in all his ways and loving toward all he has made."

God is good. One of the ways He shows His goodness is by the way He takes care of all He has made—everything in creation, including us! We call this attribute *benevolence*.

1. Choose one of these passages:

Job 38:39–39:30; Psalm 104; Psalm 116; Psalm 139:1–18; Psalm 145

2. Read the passage several times, thinking about what it says about God. Especially look for evidence of God's benevolence.

3. Write a paragraph to summarize what the passage says about God's benevolence.

Answers will vary.

4. Share your discoveries with other students.

Let God Be GOD

Interact 12.3
Does God's Goodness Matter?

Listed below are several facts. After each fact you will find two statements. These statements represent two ways of interpreting those facts. Which statements make the most sense to you? How would you explain why they make sense?

Fact: Sometimes it rains; sometimes it doesn't.

1. Wind, moisture, temperature, and other factors combine to make rain. Often we can predict when and where it will rain, but sometimes we guess wrong. The whole process is random.

2. The patterns and movements we see on weather maps are evidence that the earth's systems have an order that God built into creation. Even if we can't exactly forecast every weather change, weather systems are generally predictable. This points to a Creator.

Fact: Animals come in a wide variety of sizes, colors, and shapes. They eat a wide variety of things. They live in a wide variety of conditions, from the frozen Arctic to the burning Sahara.

1. The variety we see is basically a result of random events and accidents.

2. This variety is evidence of God's great creativity and love of beauty. The more we learn about these creatures and understand how they live, the more we admire and appreciate God's generous provision.

Fact: When people go through hard times, some pray for God's help and some get through on their own.

1. All we have is ourselves. Pray if you want to, but there's no one there to help you.

2. God gives us the strength to make it, whether we admit it or not. Praying isn't being lazy; it's facing the fact that no matter how hard we try, we all need help.

Answers will vary.

148

Let God Be GOD

Interact 12.4

Reflecting God's Goodness

Look up the following Scripture passages. Complete the chart by answering the questions for each Scripture passage.

Scripture passage	Summarize what this passage says about good works.	Give specific ways we can fulfill the teachings in this passage.
Matthew 5:16	They should point people to God.	Answers will vary.
Romans 12:9, 21	They can overcome evil.	Answers will vary.
Galatians 6:9–10	If we persist, our good works will produce results.	Answers will vary.
Ephesians 2:10	God has prepared good works for us to do.	Answers will vary.
Colossians 1:10	Good works please God and bear fruit.	Answers will vary.
1 Thessalonians 5:15, 21–22	Test everything; hold on to what is good.	Answers will vary.
2 Thessalonians 2:16–17	God will strengthen and encourage us.	Answers will vary.
Titus 2:7–8	Set an example for others.	Answers will vary.
Hebrews 10:24	We should stimulate each other to do good works.	Answers will vary.
Hebrews 13:16	God is pleased when we do good and share with others.	Answers will vary.
1 Peter 2:12, 15	Our good works should point people to God and silence evil people.	Answers will vary.
1 Peter 38–11	Be a blessing, and you will inherit a blessing.	Answers will vary.
1 Peter 4:19	Continue to do good, even if you suffer for it.	Answers will vary.

Let God Be GOD

Interact 13.1
God Is Wise

Look up the following Scripture passages. After each one, make a note about how God shows His wisdom in that passage.

Hint: In some cases, you'll have to look at nearby passages in order to figure out what the passage is about.

Job 12:13   God shows wisdom and power in creation.

Psalm 104:24   God shows His wisdom in the creatures He has created.

Jeremiah 10:12   In wisdom and power God created the heavens and the earth.

Daniel 2:20–21   God gives wisdom to the wise.

Matthew 13:54   People were amazed at Jesus' wisdom and miraculous powers.

Romans 11:33   God's wisdom is beyond our understanding.

Romans 16:27   He is the only wise God.

1 Corinthians 1:25   The foolishness of God is wiser than human wisdom.

Ephesians 3:10   God displays His wisdom in saving His people, the church.

Let God Be GOD

Interact 13.2
God's Wisdom for Us

God shares His wisdom. "If any of you lacks wisdom, he should ask God, who gives generously to all without finding fault, and it will be given to him" (James 1:5). Though we can never be as wise as God, we can acquire wisdom from God.

Look up the following Scripture passages. Then fill in the chart with your answers. (Note: You may have to look in the surrounding verses in order to answer the questions.)

Scripture	Summarize the meaning of *wisdom* in this passage.	According to this passage, how does a person receive wisdom from God?
1 Kings 3:9	Discernment, distinguishing between right and wrong	Ask for it.
1 Kings 4:29–34	Proverbs, songs, scientific knowledge.	Ask for it, research, practice.
Psalm 37:30–31	Wise speech.	Word of God in the heart.
Psalm 90:12	Heart of wisdom.	Number our days.
Psalm 111:10	Good understanding.	Fear of the Lord, following His precepts.
Proverbs 11:2	Integrity.	Humility.
Hosea 14:9	Discernment.	Righteousness.
Acts 6:3	Responsible workers.	Filled with the Holy Spirit.
Acts 6:10	Persuasive witness.	The Holy Spirit.
Romans 16:19	Wise about what is good.	Obedience.
Ephesians 1:17	Revelation of God, to know Him better.	Spirit of wisdom
Colossians 1:9	Knowledge of God's will.	Prayer.
Colossians 3:16	Singing and admonishing each other.	Word of Christ dwells within.
2 Timothy 3:15	Wise for salvation.	The Scriptures.

Let God Be GOD

Interact 13.3

Becoming Wise

Your instructor will assign you one of the following chapters from Proverbs: 1, 2, 3, 4, 8, or 9.

Write your chapter number here: _____. **Answers will vary.**

Read through the following questions. Then read your chapter several times. As you read your chapter, jot down answers to the questions. Write your answers on a separate sheet of paper.

After you have written answers to the questions, summarize the answers and transfer them to this Interact. Share your answer summaries with at least one other student.

Questions for your Proverbs chapter:

1. What synonyms did you find for *wisdom* or *wise*? What other words do these synonyms remind you of?

2. What antonyms did you find for *wisdom* or *wise*? What other words do these antonyms remind you of?

3. Why is wisdom important? What are some of the benefits of wisdom?

4. What warnings did you find?

5. What advice or guidance did you find regarding how to get wisdom?

6. How does the author link our wisdom with our relationship to God?

Let God Be GOD

My Wisdom Plan

Why it is important for me to acquire God's wisdom: **Answers will vary.**

Ways my relationship to God affects how wise I become:

Obstacles to wisdom that I must remove from my life:

Specific activities and practices that will help develop godly wisdom in my life:

Interact 13.5
God Is Truthful

Look up the following Scripture passages. Decide whether the passage is talking primarily about God's *person* or about His *words* or *both*, and check the appropriate box. Then add any notes or comments about why this information is important for us to know.

Scripture	Person or Words?		Notes
Psalm 25:5	☑ Person	☑ Words	**Answers will vary.**
Psalm 33:4	☑ Person	☑ Words	
Psalm 119:142	☐ Person	☑ Words	
Isaiah 45:19	☐ Person	☑ Words	
Daniel 9:13	☐ Person	☑ Words	
John 14:6	☑ Person	☐ Words	
John 15:26	☑ Person	☐ Words	
John 16:13	☑ Person	☑ Words	
John 17:17	☐ Person	☑ Words	
Ephesians 1:13	☐ Person	☑ Words	
2 Timothy 2:25	☐ Person	☑ Words	
2 Timothy 4:4	☐ Person	☑ Words	
Titus 1:1	☐ Person	☑ Words	
James 1:18	☐ Person	☑ Words	
1 John 5:20	☑ Person	☐ Words	
Revelation 3:7	☑ Person	☐ Words	
Revelation 15:3	☑ Person	☐ Words	
Revelation 19:9	☐ Person	☑ Words	
Revelation 19:11	☑ Person	☐ Words	
Revelation 21:5	☐ Person	☑ Words	

Let God Be GOD

Interact 13.6
Reflecting God's Truthfulness

Look up the following Scripture passages. Complete the chart by answering the questions for each Scripture passage. (Note: You may want to look at the surrounding verses to get a better understanding of the passage.)

Scripture passage	Summarize what this passage says about reflecting God's truthfulness.	Give specific ways we can fulfill the teachings in this passage.
Psalm 15	Answers will vary.	
Proverbs 12:17		
Proverbs 22:17–21		
Proverbs 23:23		
Isaiah 59:14–15		
Zechariah 8:16–17		
Proverbs 11:1, 16:11		
John 19:35, 21:24		
1 Corinthians 13:6		
Ephesians 4:15, 25		
Ephesians 6:14		
Philippians 4:8		
1 John 1:1–3		
1 John 1:6		
1 John 3:18		
2 John 1–4		
3 John 3–4		

Interact 14.1
God Is Holy

Complete a Scripture search. Look up and read the passage assigned to you. Complete the Interact. For each passage, supply the following: The **problem** of the story; the teaching about God's **holiness**; the teaching about human **sinfulness**; and a specific, personal, and measurable **application** for your life today.

Leviticus 10:1–11

Problem   Profane (unauthorized) fire was offered to God.

Holiness   If God is holy, He needs mediators, "go-betweens," or priests who are set apart (Leviticus 21). The restrictions and rules were rigid for these spiritual leaders because these people were to reflect God's character.

Sinfulness   God established specific instructions for burning incense before Him (Leviticus 9). Violating those instructions was sin and resulted in severe punishment, even death.

Application   The priests who offered incense before God were responsible for following His instructions. More responsibility brings greater accountability.

Leviticus 24:10–23

Problem   Blasphemy (taking God's name in vain).

Holiness   God's name reflects His nature, character, or person. To defame or take lightly the name of God is to detract from God Himself.

Sinfulness   To take God's name in vain means to make it mean nothing, to trivialize its importance. People do this by not meaning what they say about God—giving "lip service" but not literal service.

Application   We are accountable for what we say and don't say.

 Interact 14.1 Continued

Joshua 7

Problem   Achan took from Jericho what was forbidden.

Holiness   God means what He says. There are no exceptions.

Sinfulness   No one is above the rules. The law applies to all. Breaking laws affects those who may be innocent (7:3–5).

Application   ne person's disobedience negatively affects the whole group.

2 Samuel 6:1–8

Problem   Uzzah touched the ark of the covenant, and God had forbidden such an action (Numbers 4:4, 15–20).

Holiness   Sometimes we may take God's holiness for granted. Honor and majesty are due God alone, regardless of our views on the matter.

Sinfulness   Many argue that God is too harsh here. "He only touched it," they'll say. In fairness, our next breath is a gift from God. He owes us nothing.

Application   Our view of sin is too light; our view of God is too low. There are no little sins (Matthew 12:36).

Let God Be GOD

Acts 5:1–11

Problem   Ananias and Sapphira lied to God.

Holiness   God's standards are immutable.

Sinfulness   At the beginning of the church, God wanted people to know and fear Him (Acts 5:5, 11; 9:31).

Application   If there were no judgment for sin, right and wrong wouldn't matter. Judgment begins with believers (1 Peter 4:17).

Acts 12:19–23

Problem   Herod accepted acclaim from the crowd that he was a god.

Holiness   Only God deserves to be called God.

Sinfulness   Since Genesis 3, people have wanted to usurp God's position.

Application   In our desire to be great, pride and self-exaltation only serve to lower us.

Let God Be GOD

Interact 14.2

God Is Righteous

Look up the following Scripture passages and answer the questions. Be prepared to discuss your answers in class.

1. Once in a while, the Bible describes certain people as righteous. According to these verses, why are some people called righteous?

Genesis 18:22–25 **Exodus 9:27** **1 Samuel 24:17** **Psalm 15:1–2** **Psalm 97:10–12** **Psalm 103:17–18** **Psalm 112:1–9** **Proverbs 16:12**	Answers will vary.

2. Righteousness is an attribute of God. According to these verses, how does God show that He is righteous?

Psalm 7:9 **Psalm 31:1** **Psalm 51:14** **Psalm 65:5** **Psalm 116:5** **Psalm 119:40** **Psalm 143:1, 11** **Isaiah 45:23–25**	Answers will vary.

3. Read these New Testament verses and answer the questions.

Matthew 5:20 **Luke 5:31–32** **Luke 18:9** **John 17:25** **Romans 1:17** **Romans 3:10** **Romans 3:20–22** **Romans 4:13** **2 Corinthians 5:21** **Philippians 3:8–9**	Answers will vary.

What kind of righteousness does God demand of us? How is it possible for us to have that kind of righteousness? What makes it possible for us to be righteous? Why is it dangerous to assume that we're righteous when we're not?

Let God Be GOD

Interact 15.1
Old Testament Mercy

Read the Scripture passages and answer the questions.

1. What did Adam and Eve deserve? (Genesis 2:17)

They deserved immediate death.

What did Adam and Eve receive? (Genesis 3:17–24)

They received mercy when God allowed them to live. They were driven from the garden, but received long life and an opportunity for renewed fellowship with God outside the garden.

2. What did Cain deserve? (Genesis 4:10–12)

Cain deserved death for killing his brother.

What did Cain receive? (Genesis 4:13–16)

He would live, but he would be a fugitive. God gave him a "mark" so that others would not kill him.

3. What did humans deserve? (Genesis 6:5–7)

They deserved death for rebellion against God.

What did humans receive? (Genesis 6:3, 8)

God chose Noah as His means of preserving humanity.

4. What did the Amorites deserve? (Genesis 15:16)

They deserved judgment.

What did the Amorites receive? (Genesis 15:16)

God gave them four more generations to repent, noting that their sin "has not yet reached its full measure."

5. What did Ahab deserve? (1 Kings 21:17–26)

He deserved death.

What did Ahab receive? (1 Kings 21:27–29)

Because of Ahab's humiliation and repentance his sentence was delayed.

6. What do believers deserve? (Psalm 103:10)

Punishment for our sins.

What do believers receive? (Psalm 103:11–14)

God's mercy; our sins are removed from us, as far as the east is from the west.

Let God Be GOD

Interact 15.2
Justice and Mercy

Read Isaiah 58 and 59 once without stopping. Then go back and read selected verses and answer these questions.

1. Why did the people think themselves religious? (58:1–3)
They sought God and seemed eager to know God's ways and to have God be close to them; they even fasted.

2. What specific items did the Lord identify in the people's conduct that showed their religion to be corrupt? (58:3–14)
The Lord identified deeds of injustice and failure to extend mercy.

3. What did the Lord identify as actions that would demonstrate true religion? (58:6–14)
Practicing justice; ridding themselves of oppression; showing mercy by sharing food, clothes, and shelter.

4. What would be the results if the actions listed for question 3 were followed? (58:8–14)
There would be healing, righteousness, God's protection, and answers to prayer; Judah's "light will rise"; God would satisfy their needs and guide their ways; the people would delight in the Lord.

5. List metaphors, similes, and other word pictures that God uses to describe the people's sin. (59:1–11) Why are these word pictures used?
Hands stained with blood, fingers stained with guilt, lips have spoken lies, tongue mutters wicked things, hatch the eggs of vipers, spin a spider's web, feet rush to sin, swift to shed innocent blood, their paths are crooked roads, grope like blind people, growl like bears, mourn like doves, etc.

6. Underline the word *justice* in Isaiah 59:1–15. List the words that parallel *justice*. (For example, in verse 4: "No one calls for justice; no one pleads his case with integrity.") Why are these other words important?
Some other words are integrity, peace, righteousness, light, deliverance, and truth. These other words enhance the message and give it depth.

Let God Be GOD

Interact 15.2 Continued

7. List specific offenses in 59:12–15. Paraphrase the verses or describe the offenses in your own words, showing how they apply to our lives today. (For example, for "rebellion and treachery against the Lord" in verse 13, you might say, "We know what is right and refuse to do it. We plot. We find ways to get around God's standards of righteousness."

- "rebellion and treachery against the Lord, turning our backs on our God." We refuse to obey His commands.

- "fomenting oppression and revolt." We encourage rebellion in others.

- "uttering lies our hearts have conceived." We will invent any excuse to avoid obedience.

- "justice is driven back, and righteousness stands at a distance." Injustice and oppression become normal.

- "truth has stumbled in the streets, honesty cannot enter." No one is committed to the truth; people say what is convenient, what they think will benefit them.

- "truth is nowhere to be found." Everything is relative; there are no absolute standards.

- "whoever shuns evil becomes a prey." Those who follow God become victims; all society is against them.

Let God Be GOD

Interact 15.3
New Testament Justice

1. After reading each of the following passages from Matthew, circle the appropriate topic and write a word or phrase relating what Jesus said about *anger* 😠, *justice* ⚖️, or *hell* 😈.

5:21–22 _____

7:1–2 _____

7:13–14 _____

10:28 _____

11:20–24 _____

12:35–37 _____

13:47–51 _____

16:21–23 _____

18:6 _____

21:18–22 _____

21:33–46 _____

25:28–30 _____

2. Why doesn't God punish evil and evildoers now?

Answers will vary.

Let God Be GOD

Interact 16.1
God's Wrath

Read each section of Scripture and record what it says about God's judgment and wrath.

The Lord Judges

Deuteronomy 32:35–36

Judgment belongs to the Lord; He will avenge in due time.

2 Thessalonians 1:5–10

God will judge; He will pay back trouble.

2 Peter 3:8–10

The day of the Lord's judgment will come when people least expect it.

Revelation 20:11–15

God will judge according to what is written in the Book of Life.

The Lord's Wrath

Isaiah 34:8

The day of the Lord's vengeance will come.

Isaiah 61:2

The day of the Lord's vengeance will come.

Romans 1:18–23

God's wrath is against the godlessness and wickedness of people who suppress the truth.

Hebrews 10:28–31

Those who reject Jesus will be punished; it is a fearful thing to fall into the hands of the living God.

Let God Be GOD

Interact 16.2

God's Long-Suffering

Read the following Scripture passages and complete the activities. Be prepared to discuss your answers.

1. Read Romans 2:1–11. Note any information you find regarding God's justice and patience. What further facts can we infer from what this passage teaches?

2. Read all the verses below; then answer the questions.

Exodus 34:6–7; Isaiah 48:9; Psalm 30:5; Psalm 78:38; 2 Peter 3:9; and Psalm 103:8–10.

What do we deserve?   **Death, punishment**

What do we receive?   **Mercy**

What do we forget?   **What we deserve.**

What do we expect?   **What we receive.**

3. Read the verses below; then write your first impression of God's long-suffering.

Jeremiah 2:32; Jeremiah 4:22; Jeremiah 5:1; Jeremiah 5:30–31; and Jeremiah 35:12–19.

Answers will vary.

4. In 25 to 50 words, tell how you feel about God's long-suffering.

Answers will vary.

Let God Be GOD

Interact 16.3
God Is Love

1. The following Bible passages talk about the love of God. As you read each passage, write *why* the author says God is loving. (Look for actions of God that show He is loving; also look for other attributes that the writers link to God's love.)

Exodus 34:5–7

God is compassionate and gracious, slow to anger, abounding in love and faithfulness, maintaining love to thousands, and forgiving wickedness, rebellion, and sin.

Deuteronomy 7:7–8

God kept His promises and delivered His people from slavery in Egypt.

Deuteronomy 10:14–15

He chose the Hebrews as His people.

2 Chronicles 7:3

He is good, and His love endures forever.

2 Chronicles 20:21

He is good, and His love endures forever.

Ezra 3:11

He is good, and His love endures forever.

Psalm 33:4–5

God's word is right and true; He is faithful in all He does.

Psalm 36:5–10

The Lord is faithful, righteous, and just; He is a refuge; He is the fountain of life.

Psalm 103:8

He is compassionate, gracious, slow to anger, abounding in love.

Psalm 145:8

He is compassionate, gracious, slow to anger, rich in love.

Jeremiah 31:3

He has loved His people with an everlasting love; He has drawn them to Himself with loving-kindness.

Lamentations 3:22–23

His compassions never fail; they are new every morning; great is His faithfulness.

John 3:16

God gave His Son out of love for the world.

John 13:1

Jesus washed His disciples' feet.

John 17:23–26

The Father loves Jesus' followers with the same love shared by the Father and the Son.

Romans 5:8

Christ died for us while we were still sinners.

Romans 8:35–39

Nothing can separate us from God's love.

2 Corinthians 13:14

Along with the love of God, we have the grace of the Lord Jesus Christ and the fellowship of the Holy Spirit.

2. According to the passages below, how should we respond to the fact that God is love? (You may also find suggestions in the passages you looked at when answering the first question.)

Matthew 22:35–40; John 15:9–17; Ephesians 5:1–2; Philippians 2:1–2; and 1 John 4:16, 19

Answers will vary, but the most frequent responses are worship and thanksgiving.

Interact 16.4
Singing God's Love

The book of Psalms is a worship songbook. Read the following passages from Psalms. Beside each passage, make notes and comments about the verses. What does the psalm writer say about God's love? How does God's love make a difference in the writer's life? How can we live in God's love?

6:4 God delivers from trouble.

13:5 The psalmist trusts God to save him.

25:6–7 God shows mercy and love by not remembering the psalmist's past sins.

31:14–16 God saves from enemies.

42:8 God gives a song in the night.

51:1 God forgives sin.

86:5 God forgives and shows His love to those who call on Him.

89:1–2 God has been faithful through all generations.

101:1 God is loving and just.

117:1–2 God's faithfulness endures forever.

118:1–4 God's love endures forever.

136:1–26 God's love endures forever; it is displayed in creation and in God's mighty deeds on behalf of His people.

145:8 God is gracious and compassionate, slow to anger and rich in love.

Let God Be GOD

Interact 17.1

Complementary or Contradictory?

Complete this Interact by following the directions in each section.

1. Look up the following verses about God's love and God's hate. Write down the word or phrase that tells whom or what God loves or hates.

God's Love	God's Hate
Deuteronomy 4:32–38 Love motivated God to deliver His people.	**Proverbs 6:16–19** lying tongue, hands that shed innocent blood, a heart that devises wicked schemes, feet that are quick to rush into evil, a false witness who pours out lies and a man who stirs up dissension among brothers.
Deuteronomy 7:7–9 God chose His people because He loved them.	**Isaiah 1:13–15** God hates hypocritical worship.
Psalm 103:17 God loves those who fear Him.	**Isaiah 61:8** God hates robbery and iniquity.
Psalm 119:64, 124 The earth is full of God's love.	**Amos 5:21** God hates hypocritical worship.
Psalm 146:8–10 God loves the blind, those who are bowed down, the righteous, the alien, the fatherless, and the widow.	**Psalm 5:4–6** God hates evil, boastfulness, and those who practice evil.
Malachi 1:2–3 God chose His people because He loved them.	**Psalm 11:4–6** God hates the wicked and those who love violence.

2. For each verse or passage listed below, write a phrase that indicates what, whom, and how we are to love or hate. (Remember that these verses represent only a few of many that could be cited.)

Our Love	Our Hate
Deuteronomy 10:19 Answers will vary.	**Psalm 139:21** Answers will vary.
Deuteronomy 6:5 Answers will vary.	**Psalm 119:128** Answers will vary.
Deuteronomy 10:12–13 Answers will vary.	**Psalm 119:163** Answers will vary.

3. In the space below, write a short paragraph about the proper objects of our love and hate.

Answers will vary.

Let God Be GOD

Let God Be GOD

A Study of the Attributes of God | Blackline Masters | Answer Key

Mark Eckel

It matters
that God exists because ...

It **doesn't** matter
that God exists if ...

According to **our society** today, God is ...

According to **Scripture**, God is ...

Unit 1 Quiz

1. How has God revealed Himself?

General revelation (nature and conscience)

Special revelation (the Bible)

2. How can we sort through and evaluate the many different definitions of God we hear from books, TV, movies, and neighbors?

Compare them to the teachings of Scripture.

God's Attributes

Attribute	Verses	Definition	Application

Unit 2 Quiz

1. What is an attribute?

A characteristic of God.

2. How can attributes help us talk about God?

They give us words describing who He is.

3. Read Psalm 25. List all the attributes of God you find in that psalm. Write the verse number where you found each attribute.

Answers will vary.

In the beginning God created the heavens and the earth.

—Genesis 1:1

Hear, O Israel: The Lord our God, the Lord is one.

—Deuteronomy 6:4

Unit 3 Quiz

1. What is the difference between monotheism and polytheism?

Monotheism is belief in one God; polytheism is belief in more than one God.

2. What does Genesis 1:1 tell us about God?

He exists; He is all-powerful; He is eternal; He is separate from His creation; He is uncreated.

3. What does Deuteronomy 6:4 tell us about God?

God is one; He is Lord.

4. What is an idol?

Anything that takes the place of God in a person's life.

5. Why is it important to know that there is only one God?

Answers will vary.

The doctrine of the Trinity
can be summarized in these three
statements:

• There is one God.

• God is three persons:
Father, Son, and Holy Spirit.

• Each of the persons is fully God.

Unit 4 Quiz

1. Complete the blanks to describe the Trinity.

• There is one God.

• God is three persons: Father, Son, and Holy Spirit.

• Each of the persons is fully God.

2. Give two reasons why it's important that God is a Trinity.

God is love, and has been throughout eternity.

Because Jesus is God, He was able to make atonement for our sins.

I am the Lord, and there is no other;
apart from me there is no God.

—Isaiah 45:5

Unit 5 Quiz

1. What do we mean when we say that God is supreme?

He is high above every other "god."

2. What difference does it make in our daily life to know that God is supreme?

Answers will vary.

3. What do we mean when we say that God is self–existent?

He did not have a beginning; He depends on nothing else for His existence; He is independent of His creation.

4. What difference does it make in our daily life to know that God is self–existent?

Answers will vary.

God designs possibilities; He is not interested in each detail of life.

God is caught off guard by world situations, which change so quickly that He must change His plans.

Humans control their own destiny.

If God is not sovereign, then God is not God. If there is any element of the universe that is outside of his authority, then he no longer is God over all. In other words, sovereignty belongs to deity. Sovereignty is a natural attribute of the Creator. God owns what he makes, and he rules what he owns.

—R. C. Sproul

Sovereignty
God has everything under control.
(There are no emergencies in heaven.)

Providence
God cares for and
personally oversees all events.
(There is no accident or coincidence,
no chance or luck, with God.)

Are there areas in my life in which I resist God's sovereign control? What are they?

What would it be like if God were not involved in who I am? Would I prefer it that way?

If God is in control of all things, why does He allow bad things to happen?

Unit 6 Quiz

1. What do we mean when we say that God is sovereign?

God has ultimate authority over every created being.

2. What can the book of Job teach us about God's sovereignty?

God is absolute ruler; we must trust Him even though we don't understand His ways; answers will vary.

Let God Be GOD   **BLM 6.5**

Let God Be GOD   **BLM 7.1**

Unit 7 Quiz

1. What two meanings of *infinite* do we use when we apply the word to God?

"Unlimited" and "perfect."

2. Why can there be only one infinite being?

Another infinite being would limit the first one; therefore, neither would be unlimited.

TIMEless

Time Created After Eternal Planning

Heaven (UPI). After the project had been an eternity on the drawing board, the Trinity created time, space, and matter (Genesis 1:1). Future physics students will be glad for this balance in creation.

Time defined: Just as distance is the space between two places, time is the space between two events. The regularity and predictability of these events provide the basis for all measurement concepts of time—such as minute, hour, day, and year.

Newsflash!

Jerusalem (AP). A thousand years is like a day to God. According to Psalm 90:4, God apparently has a different timekeeping scale than humans. He is quoted as stating that for each of His heavenly days, 1,000 human years pass. That's about a 365,000:1 ratio of earthly to heavenly days.

Lifespan Shortened

Palestine (AP). Scientists discovered today that the length of one's life can be compared to the longevity of fog on a sunny day (James 4:14).

Daylight Working Hours

Rome (AP). According to sources, employers are urging that production quotas be increased because night is coming up very soon (Romans 13:12).

Time Trials Begin

Damascus (AP). Paul announced that the race of the Christian life continues, according to a source quoted in 1 Corinthians 9:24–29. When asked, he commented, "Those who race in the Roman races do it for a crown that will not last, but we do it to get a crown that will last forever—a crown of life."

Obituaries

Rome. Joe Citizen, DOB 05.30.42, died yesterday in a Roman arena from mortal wounds delivered by a lion, three bulls, a bear, and a Roman animal trainer. Funeral services will be held tomorrow at the home of Mr. Citizen. The burial will be in the Unmarked Cemetery for Jewish Martyrs. Joe is survived by his wife and children.

Special note to our readers: TIMEless will cease this obituary column at the end of time.

Unit 8 Quiz

1. Read Malachi 3:6. According to this verse, why is it a good thing that God is immutable?

Israel was not destroyed.

2. Read Exodus 32:9–14. In this passage, God seems to change His mind. What might be a better explanation of God's actions in this passage?

God was expressing something that is beyond our comprehension; He speaks in human terms (anthropomorphism).

3. A friend says to you, "We live in time. What's so important about believing that God is eternal?" Write an answer to your friend.

Answers will vary.

Let God Be GOD   **BLM 8.2**

If God is **incomprehensible**, why should we study about Him?

Unit 9 Quiz

1. What do we mean when we say that God is incomprehensible? Does it mean we can know nothing about Him?

It means we cannot know Him fully or completely.

2. Read Psalm 62. What does the psalmist know about God? List the characteristics of God you find in this psalm.

Answers will vary.

3. We cannot describe God perfectly (He is ineffable), but there is a lot we can say about Him. Sometimes the Bible writers make direct statements about God; sometimes they use figurative language. Read Psalm 62 again, and list the metaphors for God you find in this psalm.

Answers will vary.

Let God Be GOD   BLM 9.2

O Lord, you have searched me and you know me.

—Psalm 139:1

Unit 10 Quiz

1. What does the word *omniscient* mean?

God knows everything.

2. What effect does God's omniscience have on your life?

Answers will vary.

3. What does the word *omnipresent* mean?

God is fully present everywhere.

4. What effect does God's omnipresence have on your life?

Answers will vary.

God's Power Questions

In Job 38–41, God asked Job lots of questions in order to remind Job, "You are not God!"

Use the following question starters to create your own questions that God might want to ask us.

Who are you?   What did you …?   Can you even imagine …?

Have you ever …?   Do you know …?   Can you tell Me …?

When did you …?   Are you able to …?   Do you have control over …?

Did you …?   Do you really think you …?

Unit 11 Quiz

1. What do we mean when we say that God is omnipotent?

God is all-powerful

2. What does the natural world reveal about God's power?

Answers will vary.

3. How did Jesus reveal His power when He was on earth?

Miracles, conquest of sin, resurrection.

4. When we observe God's power, how should we respond?

Answers will vary.

Let God Be GOD   BLM 11.2

Is God Good?

Yes	Other Views

Unit 12 Quiz

1. How does God demonstrate that He is good?

By what He does.

2. How does God take care of His creation? What do we call this special kind of goodness of God?

Provides for living things (answers will vary); benevolence.

3. Describe three specific things we can do to reflect God's goodness.

Answers will vary.

WISDOM MATTERS!

God says ...

Others say ...

Unit 13 Quiz

1. How does God display His wisdom?

In creation; in His actions; in His Word.

2. Why is it important to know that God is truthful?

We can trust what He says; He will be faithful to fulfill His promises.

3. How can we reflect God's wisdom and truthfulness?

Answers will vary.

Be Holy

Speak to the entire assembly of Israel and say to them: "Be holy because I, the Lord your God, am holy."

—Leviticus 19:2

Exalt the Lord our God
and worship at his holy mountain,
for the Lord our God is holy.

—Psalm 99:9

But just as he who called you is holy, so be holy in all you do.

—1 Peter 1:15

Unit 14 Quiz

1. What do we mean when we say that God is holy?

God is totally separate from His creation; He is without sin.

2. In 1 Peter 1:16, Peter quotes God: "Be holy, because I am holy." Give two examples of ways we can obey this command.

Answers will vary.

3. What do we mean when we say that God is righteous?

God does what is right and sets the standards for what is right.

4. How can we reflect God's righteousness?

Answers will vary.

Unit 15 Quiz

1. What do we mean when we say that God is just?

God is fair; He acts according to His just laws.

2. What do we mean when we say that God is merciful?

He does not punish us as we deserve.

3. Why is it important for us that God is both just and merciful?

Answers will vary.

4. How can we reflect God's justice and mercy?

Answers will vary.

We are punished justly, for we are getting what our deeds deserve. But this man has done nothing wrong.

—Luke 23:41

Unit 16 Quiz

1. How is God's wrath related to His long-suffering?

He does not act immediately on His wrath; He delays His judgment.

2. What do we mean when we say that God is love?

God is love in His very being; the members of the Trinity have an eternal love relationship.

3. How does the doctrine of the Trinity relate to God's love?

God has always been love, even before anything was created.

4. How can we reflect God's long-suffering and love?

Answers will vary.

What Do You Think?

- God's love should be emphasized over His hate.

- God cannot hate.

- Christians are to love the sinner but hate the sin.

- We should not fear God.

- God is loving. He would not allow anyone to go to hell.

Complementary Attributes

Unit 17 Quiz

1. Choose one of these pairs of attributes, and write a short definition of each one.

Patience	Love	Mercy	Judgment
Wrath	Hate	Justice	Forgiveness

Patience. God withholds His judgment.

Wrath. God is angry against sin.

Love. The three persons of the Trinity relate to each other in love.

Hate. God detests sin.

Mercy. God does not give us what we deserve.

Justice. God is always fair and just.

Judgment. God will judge sinners.

Forgiveness. God forgives the sins of those who confess their sin.

2. Explain why those two attributes are complementary rather than contradictory.

Answers will vary.

Course Evaluation

This evaluation will help me, the teacher, do a better job the next time I teach this course. Please answer honestly, and do not put your name on the evaluation. This evaluation will not be read until AFTER final grades are completed and turned in.

What part of the course did you like best? Why?

Which lesson or topic was the most interesting and enjoyable? Why?

Which lesson or topic was the most meaningful or helpful to you? Why?

If you could change anything about the overall course, what would it be?

One strength of my teacher is:

One weakness of my teacher is:

Did the class meet the goals set forth at the beginning of the semester? If not, why not?

What kinds of changes would benefit the next group of students to take this course?

Final Commitment

This paper will not be collected or seen by anyone except you. Please be honest in filling out this form. Your honesty will allow God to use this commitment and the things you have learned to help you grow toward real maturity in Christ.

The one truth that had the biggest impact on my life is:

An area of my life that I need to improve or in which I need to grow is:

An area of my life about which I feel confident when I consider the character of God is:

After studying the nature of God, I feel:

I am willing to commit myself to a closer relationship with God.   Yes   No